THE USE OF THE BIBLE IN MILTON'S PROSE

THE USE OF THE BIBLE IN MILTON'S PROSE

WITH

AN INDEX OF THE BIBLICAL QUOTATIONS AND CITATIONS ARRANGED IN THE CHRONOLOGICAL ORDER OF THE PROSE WORKS; ANOTHER INDEX OF ALL QUOTATIONS AND CITATIONS IN THE ORDER OF THE BOOKS OF THE BIBLE; AND AN INDEX OF THE QUOTATIONS AND CITATIONS IN THE *De Doctrina*

HARRIS FRANCIS FLETCHER
*Assistant Professor of English
The University of Illinois*

HASKELL HOUSE PUBLISHERS LTD.
Publishers of Scarce Scholarly Books
NEW YORK, N. Y. 10012
1970

821
M71 ZfL

First Published 1929

HASKELL HOUSE PUBLISHERS Ltd.
Publishers of Scarce Scholarly Books
280 LAFAYETTE STREET
NEW YORK, N. Y. 10012

Library of Congress Catalog Card Number: 75-95425

Standard Book Number 8383-0974-7

Printed in the United States of America

FOREWORD

This work is the direct result of the need for fuller information and more complete apparatus with which to study more closely Milton's quotation and citation of the Bible. The discussion of the various editions and texts of the Bible ordinarily employed by Milton seemed valuable after analysis of the entire mass of his Biblical citations in all his prose including the *De Doctrina*. It brings together some hitherto scattered information concerning those texts and versions, and adds several new facts about Milton's use of the Bible.

It is hoped that the indices included here will prove as helpful to other students of Milton as they have already proved to the compiler. It is unfortunate that there is no standard edition of Milton's works that includes the *De Doctrina*. But by using Mitford for all the prose except the *De Doctrina* and Summer's admirable edition of that work, it has been possible to make a reference to every Biblical citation or quotation in Milton's prose.

Thanks are due to Professors Edward Chauncey Baldwin, George Tobias Flom, William Abbott Oldfather, and Jacob Zeitlin for having read this work in manuscript, and for making many valuable suggestions.

Despite many checkings and considerable use of the tables, the compiler fears that in so many chapter-verse references there may be errors. He would be grateful to have all such errors called to his attention.

HARRIS FRANCIS FLETCHER

URBANA, Illinois
October, 1929.

TABLE OF CONTENTS

CHAPTER I

INTRODUCTION

As subjects of special study, Milton's knowledge and use of the Bible have been almost completely neglected by scholars and students of his work, Thompson's *Bibliography*,[1] which of course records none of the activity in Milton scholarship of the past fifteen years, failing even to note "Bible" as a topic-heading. The years since the appearance of this *Bibliography* have produced almost nothing specifically dealing with such subjects. Even for the poetry, though sporadic attention has been accorded the appearance in it of all manner of fragments, both of ideas and of phrases, traceable directly to his Biblical reading, such material has never been systematized, nor has it in itself received any special attention. Although commentators on his poetry have been especially active in generally pointing out his indebtedness directly to the Bible for a great many details found in his work, all schematic and much useful information is lacking. The great annotated editions, Hume's, Bentley's, Newton's, Warton's, Todd's, Masson's, and Verity's, impress us throughout their notes by their constant reference to the Old or New Testament, but always reference that is for the scholar indeterminate and unsatisfactory. Biographers from Phillips to Trent have, in connection with his poetry, spoken frequently of Milton's familiarity with Scripture, Masson perhaps as in so many other respects supplying us with more detailed and adequate information about the general subject than the others; but even he leaves much to be said.

If, scattered throughout the works of his biographers and poetical annotators, there is fair recognition of his use of the Bible in his poetry, nevertheless, there is nowhere a study either precise or definite that informs the student with respect to the most elemental questions concerned with the form of Scripture Milton most frequently employed. While it has been generally accepted that Milton knew the Bible intimately and throughout his lifetime, very little beyond this unverified generality is known of his pre-

[1] Thompson, E. N. S., *John Milton Topical Bibliography*, New Haven, 1916.

9

cise knowledge and use of what is obviously one of the most important of all books that are or may be connected with him.

So far as his prose works are concerned, the lack of definite information concerning his use of the Bible is even more striking. No detailed or in any way complete study of his use of the Bible in them has ever appeared, the only accounts of consequence, both incomplete, being one by Sumner, included in his *Introduction* to his translation of the *Christian Doctrine*, and my brief survey of a few years ago.[2]

The importance of systematic study of Milton's use of the Bible in his prose works is very great. In them, as contrasted with the poetry, there is first of all the information to be gained from the immense number of exact chapter and verse citations impossible to obtain from the poetry. In addition to this information, there is also that afforded by the direct and indirect quotations to be found in the prose, usually with some typographical indications of what Milton felt to be quotations and what not. These indications of quotation are a great help in considering his use of the Bible, and appear only in the prose. All these chapter and verse citations together with the carefully indicated quotations are of direct importance throughout the prose works, although rather too obvious to be more than mentioned here.

Equally important, and almost equally obvious, is the fact that a virtually complete knowledge of all phases of Milton's Bible study may be gained by an exhaustive investigation of his use of the Bible in his prose. This makes the subject important in itself, and not for secondary or derived reasons. The usefulness as a tool of a complete digest of the Biblical citations and quotations in the prose works is at once apparent. Such a digest is as valuable as a concordance or a listing of references of any kind whatever.

Moreover, there is in an age like our own that reads the Bible but little, great value to be attached to a study which helps us to realize how saturated with Scripture were the life and learning of Milton's day. We have, at least the rank and file of us today, forgotten how greatly dependent upon Biblical study was all learning in Western Europe of ages previous to our own. Most if not quite all scholarship of the seventeenth century still centered in Biblical studies. Thus Milton's knowledge of the Bible constitutes in

[2] "Milton's Use of Biblical Quotations," *Journal of English and Germanic Philology*, XXVI (1927) pp. 145–165.

many ways a criterion of his general learning and scholarship,
as the same factor did for other scholars of his time. Because this
is less true today than at any other period in the past fifteen hundred years, the study of Milton's use of the Bible is valuable in
recalling to us how inevitable a thorough knowledge of that work
was to the trained scholar of the time. In many ways Milton's
knowledge and use of the Bible may be regarded as a sort of meas-
uring-rod of his general learning. Between his knowledge and use
of the Bible and his knowledge and use of the classics, his whole
intellectual training and outlook will be comprehended in so far
as they ever may be.

Directly dependent upon the degree of familiarity with the Bible
is such a question as his acquaintance with the rabbis in their original Hebrew. Such acquaintance rests primarily upon his knowledge of Hebrew תנך (*Tenach, i.e.,* Hebrew text of the Old Testament) and Aramaic Targums in their respective originals. His
acquaintance with these directly has been too generally assumed,
without detailed proof.[3] Such proof is contained almost entirely
in his own uses of the text of Scripture, that is, in instances he himself provides of his actual employment of Hebrew text or Aramaic
Targum.

As an aid directly to our understanding of the Latin *de doctrina*,
a knowledge of its author's use of the Bible therein is indispensable.
This posthumously printed work, long unknown to Milton scholars,
must be understood first of all in connection with its employment
of Scripture. According to its author, it is a system of theology based
exclusively on the Bible, and although we soon discover that this is
not strictly true, it is nevertheless imperative for us to understand
exactly what Milton has done with the Bible in this work. One of
the great difficulties encountered in the past when working with the
de doctrina has been occasioned by the virtual lack of all apparatus
necessary to do much with it. Aside from an excellent account of
its contents to be found in Masson's *Life*, and its use in Grierson's
remarkable digest of Milton's theology, very little has been done,
even by Saurat, with the *de doctrina* in connection with Milton's other
work, especially the poetry. And any understanding of the *de doctrina* for its own sake or for the sake of Milton's other works must
begin with its enormous use of the Bible.

[3] My recent study, *Milton's Rabbinical Readings*, rests as much on this demonstrated familiarity with *Tenach* and *Targum* in their originals as it does on any other
one basis.

Another important aspect of the study of Milton's use of the Bible in his prose works is the evidence it affords of the need for a re-evaluation of his use of the Bible in his poetry. One may well suspect, because of the uncertainty of our knowledge of his use of Scripture, that many statements and assumptions made about it in connection with his poetry are misleading and perhaps false. Many of his assumed deviations from Scripture in his poetry are due rather to our own ignorance of what Scripture meant to him. There are several flagrant cases to be found in the annotators of his poetry in which he has been charged by critic or commentator with infidelity to Scripture. If we knew more about the nature and form of the Scriptural texts used by Milton, it would perhaps be possible in many such instances to show that these charges are almost wholly due to the inadequacy of the acquaintanceship of the commentators with what Milton was actually doing.[4] Thus, it is of great importance for the annotator or editor to know more about Milton's actual knowledge of the Bible and use of it than has been known in the past. This knowledge can only be acquired through the systematic study made possible by the precise references and quotations found throughout his prose works.

This study will therefore be concerned with the investigation of how in his prose Milton used the text of Scripture and the various forms in which he knew it. Such questions as the following must be answered: What text of Scripture did he customarily use? What version or text did he consider the most authentic, and why? Was he a "literalist" so far as the text of Scripture was concerned? In order to answer this last question, we must of course be prepared to answer the question "What text?" And furthermore, did he know enough about Biblical literature to enable him to appreciate the problem of textual accuracy? Only on the basis of a rigorous treatment of such questions as those proposed, therefore, can an investigation of his Biblical uses proceed.

The method of procedure for such a study is simple enough. In order to obtain valid bases for certainty regarding Milton's practice in using Scripture, only an exhaustive examination of his use of Biblical quotations is necessary. In the English prose works, and in the Latin, especially in the posthumously published but well-authenticated *de doctrina Christiana*, appear many chapter

[4] *cf.* instances cited in my *Rabbinical Readings*, especially the "compasses" passage, *Paradise Lost* VII: 225.

and verse citations of Scripture and quotations from it. The collation of these with a Biblical text constitutes a basis for the investigation of Milton's knowledge of Scripture and employment of it which leaves nothing to be desired. As a basis for this investigation, all of the quotations appearing in Milton's prose have been collated with a Biblical text. Since Milton refers to over seven thousand Latin Biblical passages in the *de doctrina* alone, and quotes all or parts of most of these passages, there can be no quarrel with the adequacy afforded by these quotations as an indication of his use of the Bible. For purposes of collation, except for the *de doctrina*, I have used Mitford's text of the prose, supplementing this with photostatic copies of the first and an original copy of the second edition of the *Doctrine and Discipline of Divorce.*[5] For the *de doctrina*, I have used Sumner's admirable Latin edition.[6] I have most fortunately been able to compare this with the photostatic copy belonging to Columbia University of the original manuscript, prepared by Milton's amanuenses, in the Public Records office. In some cases, collation with the manuscript itself afforded a certainty which it would have been impossible to secure from any printed edition. I shall discuss Milton's use of Biblical passages in the posthumous *de doctrina* apart from his use in his other prose works, but only for convenience. For the same reason, I shall also separate his English quotations and citations of Scripture from those which appear in his Latin works other than the *de doctrina*.

[5] I wish to acknowledge with gratitude the kindness of the late Professor C. L. Powell in supplying me with his own longhand copy of the Thomason copy of the first edition in the British Museum.

[6] *Joannis Miltoni Angli de doctrina Christiana* ex schedis manuscriptis deprompsit, et typis mandari primus curavit Carolus Ricardus Sumner, Cantabrigiae, M. DCCC. XXV.

CHAPTER II

THE USE OF THE BIBLE IN THE PROSE WORKS
EXCLUSIVE OF THE *DE DOCTRINA*

A complete survey of all the prose works, except the *de doctrina* reveals Milton's use in them of about five hundred separate quotations or citations, each of which is clearly recognizable as such Besides these, there occur a large number of Scriptural ideas or phrases, too slight to indicate chapter and verse location of origin. The list of approximately five hundred includes all, or nearly all, of the passages in Milton's prose which are clearly of some definite Scriptural origin.

These passages will be found listed in an accompanying table, arranged as they appear in the chronologically arranged prose works.[1] This table is intended to afford a very full and complete list of Milton's drawings on Scripture throughout all his prose works, excluding the *de doctrina*.

In his prose works, Milton used Scripture in several different ways. Among these may be distinguished four principal ones, which follow:

1. Citations of Scriptural passages without quotation.
2. Use of Scriptural material with no indication of origin.
3. Quotations agreeing with a definite text.
4. Quotations differing from any recognized text.
   a. Clipping.
   b. Use of marginal notes from a recognized version.
   c. Change in phrasing.
   d. Milton's own version of Scripture.
   e. Adaption to fit his context.

In Milton's use of Scriptural passages, a noticeable peculiarity is his frequent citation of Biblical passages by book and chapter, or by book, chapter, and verse, without actually quoting the passage cited. He usually cited such a passage as a support for a statement of his own, or to indicate the Scriptural location of an idea which he

[1] Chapt. IV.

14

was setting forth. Such citation without quotation is indicated in the first column of my tabulation of his citations and quotations.

1. Citations of Scriptural Passages without Quotation

A good instance of such citations used to support his own statement occurs in the *Doctrine and Discipline of Divorce*.[2] Milton had made the statement that "other nations were to the Jews impure, even to the separating of marriage." He supported this by citing Exodus 34:16; Deuteronomy 7:3, 6; Ezra 9:2; 10:10, 11; Nehemiah 13:30. Such supporting citation without quotation is frequent throughout the prose works.

Another very frequent occurrence of citation without quotation is that in which the quotation is omitted because the passage had been quoted earlier in the work. A good instance of this occurs in *Tetrachordon*. On page 211[3] Milton cited Genesis 2:24 without quotation because he had already quoted the verse in full on page 144. Omission of quotation because of previous quotation, is, then, another common practice.

A third use of citation without quotation occurs when Milton wished to indicate the Biblical source of his idea, this use being almost identical with the first except that it lacks the argumentative tone. A good instance of this manner of citation occurs in the tract, *Considerations touching the likeliest Means to Remove Hirelings out of the Church*. On page 368,[4] Milton stated that richer congregations should send some of their teachers to surrounding villages. He had been discussing the undesirability of preaching for gain, and continued:

Yet grant it needful to allow them both the Charges of thir Journey and the Hire of thir Labor, it will belong next to the Charity of richer Congregations, where most commonly they abound with Teachers, to send some of thir number to the Villages round, as the Apostles from Jerusalem sent Peter and John to the City and Villages of Samaria, Acts 8:14, 25. or as the Church at Jerusalem sent Barnabas to Antioch, chap. 11:22. and other Churches joining sent Luke to travail with Paul, 2 Cor. 8:19 though whether they had thir Charges born by the Church or no, it be not recorded.

[2] Mitford, *Works*, vol. IV: 38.
[3] Mitford, *Works*, vol. IV.
[4] Mitford, *Works*, vol. V.

Another instance of the same kind occurs in *A Treatise of Civil Power in Ecclesiastical Causes.* On page 333[5] occurs the following statement:

All prophane and licentious men, so known, can be considerd but either so without the church as never yet within it, or departed thence of thir own accord, or excommunicate: if never yet within the church, whom the apostle, and so consequently the church have naught to do to judge, as he professes 1 Cor. 5:12, then by what autoritie doth the magistrate judge, or, which is worse, compell in relation to the church? if departed of his own accord, like that lost sheep Luke 15:4, &c. the true church either with her own or any borrowd force worries him not in again, etc.

Numerous other passages employ this same device to indicate the source or sources for the particular idea Milton might be using.

2. *Use of Scriptural Material with no Indication of Origin*

Another of Milton's peculiarities is the use of material which is clearly Scriptural but is not so designated. Sometimes he actually quoted the Biblical text, and sometines he paraphrased it in a most obvious manner; but in neither case citing a specific reference. This quotation of Scripture without definite citation occurs in various forms.

The largest number of actual quotations without citation of places of origin occurs in *Eikonoklastes;* but similar quotations also appear elsewhere. A representative, but not exhaustive list of such quotations follows, the source in each case being recognizable from the fragmentary quotation:

Eikon. Mitford, *Works,* vol. III: 493, "Cain sayd unto the Lord, My iniquity is greater then I can beare, behold thou hast driv'n me this day from the face of the earth, and from thy face shall I be hid." (Gen. 4:13,14.)

ibid. p. 519. "Whosoever sheddeth mans blood, by man shall his blood be shed," (Gen. 9:6.)

ibid. p. 527, "and the beginning of his Kingdom was Babel," (Gen. 10:10.)

ibid. p. 493, "And when Esau heard the words of his Father he cry'd with an exceeding bitter cry, and said, Bless me eev'n me also O my Father" (Gen. 27:34.)

ibid. p. 494, "And Pharaoh said to Moses, The Lord is righteous, I and my people are wicked; I have sin'd against the Lord your God and against you." (Ex. 9:27.)

5 Mitford, *Works,* vol. V.

ibid. "And Balaam said, Let me die the death of the righteous and let my last end be like his." (Num. 23:10.)

ibid. p. 490, "Now know I that the Lord will doe mee good seeing I have a Levite to my Priest." (Judges 17:13.)

ibid. "Yee have tak'n away my Gods which I made, and the Priest, and what have I more?" (Judges 18:24.)

ibid. p. 494, "And Saul said to Samuel, I have sin'd, for I have transgress'd the commandment of the Lord;" (1 Sam. 15:24.)

ibid. "Yet honour mee now I pray thee before the Elders of my People." (1 Sam. 15:30.)

ibid. p. 393, "God, saith he, hath deliver'd him into my hands, for he is shut in." (1 Sam. 23:7.)

ibid. "And when Ahab heard the words of Eliah, he rent his cloaths and put sackcloth upon his flesh, and fasted, and lay in sackcloth, and went softly." (1 Kings 21:27.)

Eikon. p. 494, "Jehoram also rent his cloaths, and the people look'd, and behold he had sackcloth upon his flesh, ... God doe so, and more also to me, if the head of Elishah shall stand on him this day." (2 Kings 6:30, 31.)

Reason of Church Government, vol. III: 136, "Now for a long season, Israel hath beene without the true God, and without a teaching Priest, and without law: and in those times there was no peace to him that went out, nor to him that came in, but great vexations were upon all the inhabitants of the countries. And nation was destroy'd of nation, and City of City, for God did vex them with all adversity. Be ye strong therefore, and let not your hands be weake, for your worke shall bee rewarded." (2 Chron. 15:3, 5, 6, 7.)

ibid. p. 529, "This was that King Ahaz." (2 Chron. 28:22.)

ibid. "when God slew them, then sought him;" (Psalms 78:34.)

ibid. "flatter him with thir mouth, and ly'd to him with thir tongues; for thir heart was not right with him." (Psalms 78:36, 37.)

ibid. p. 520, "Touch not mine anointed," (Psalms 105:15.)

ibid. p. 527, "To bind thir Kings in chaines, and thir Nobles with links of Iron," (Psalms 149:8.)

Reason of Church Government, p. 136, "no peace to him that went out or came in, for I, saith God, had set all men every one against his neighbor." (Zechariah 8:10.)

Eikon. p. 494, "I have sin'd, in that I have betray'd innocent blood." (Matt. 27:4.)

ibid. "Pray yee to the Lord for me that none of these things come upon me." (Acts 8:24.)

ibid. p. 527, (garblings of phrases from Rev. 17:2, 16; 18:9; and 19:21, but no citations.)

But not all his uses of Scriptural passages without citations are in the form of actual quotations. Often Milton paraphrased Scripture in an obvious way and without providing a definite reference to the passage he was paraphrasing. A few examples of this will suffice:

Of Reformation, vol. III: 4, "Such was Peters unseasonable Humilitie, as then his Knowledge was small, when Christ came to wash his feet; who at an impertinent time would needs straine courtesy with his Master, and falling troublesomly upon the lowly, alwise, and unexaminable intention of Christ in what he went with resolution to doe, so provok't by his interruption the meeke Lord, that he threat'nd to exclude him from his heavenly Portion, unlesse he could be content to be lesse arrogant, and stiff neckt in his humility," (John 13:6–10.)

Of Prelatical Episcopacy, ibid. p. 92, "for Christ hath pronounc't that no tittle of his word shall fall to the ground, and if one jot be alterable it is as possible that all should perish;" (Matt. 5:18.)

ibid. p. 84, "many of which Christ hath profest, yea though they had cast out Divells in his name, he will not know at the last day" (Matt. 7:22, 23.)

Milton sometimes used definite passages from Scripture without specific reference in still another way. This was when he quoted a text itself or recognizably paraphrased one, then added enough information to indicate the approximate origin. Sometimes he gave the name of the book and the number of the chapter, as in the following:

Eikon. p. 487, "He powreth contempt upon Princes and causeth them to wander in the Wilderness where there is no way, Psal. 107" (:40.)

Of Prel. Episc. p. 80, "the Spirit of God in Salomon . . . . My Son, saith he, honour God & the King;" (Prov. 24:21.)

Of Reformation, p. 22, "to fulfill . . . . the Prophesie of Zachariah: And it shall be that that which is in the bridle shall be holy to the Lord." (Zech. 14:20.)

Eikon. p. 515, "the plaine teaching of Christ, that no man can serve two Maisters." (Matt. 6:24, Luke 16:13.)

Paraphrastic renderings of partially indicated Biblical passages
are also common. In them Milton usually supplies enough of the
substance of the text to enable us to discover the precise passage
he was using. His mention of the book or general location in the
Bible in which the original material occurred is usually insufficient
in itself to furnish precise location. Instances of this follow:

Eikon. pp. 516–517, "It happn'd once, as we find in Esdras" (follows a
lengthy account of the material found in the third and fourth chapters of
1 Esdras.)

Of Prel. Episc. p. 92, "but an Angell from Heaven should beare us downe
that there bee three, Saint Paul has doom'd him twise, let him be accur'st,"
(Gal. 1:8.)

Of Reformation, p. 4, "the Seale of filiall grace became the Subject of horror,
and glouting adoration, pageanted about, like a dreadfull Idol: which
sometimes deceve's wel-meaning men, and beguiles them of their reward,
by their voluntary humility, which indeed, is fleshy pride, preferring a
foolish Sacrifice, and the rudiments of the world, as Saint Paul to the
Colossians explaineth, before a savory obedience to Christs example."
(Col. 2:8, 18.)

Of Prel. Episc. p. 76, "this tradition of Bishoping Timothy over Ephesus
was but taken for granted out of that place in St. Paul, which was only an
intreating him to tarry at Ephesus, to do something left him in charge."
(1 Tim. 1:3.)

ibid. p. 73, "yet to verify that which Saint Paul foretold of succeeding times,
when men began to have itching eares, then not contented with the plenti-
full and wholsom.fountaines of the Gospell, they began after their owne
lusts to heap to themselvs teachers," (2 Tim. 4:3.)

Reason of Church Government, p. 106, "Neverthelesse when Christ by those
visions of S. Iohn foreshewes the reformation of his Church, he bids him
take his Reed, and meet it out againe after the first patterne, for he prescribes him no other. Arise, said the Angell and measure the Temple of
God and the Altar, and them that worship therein." (Rev. 11:1.)

Many times in the prose works, Milton referred to the Gospels by
such a phrase as "Christ said," or some other expression using the
name Christ and indicating one of his sayings. The Pauline Epistles
were often indiscriminately referred to as "Saint Paul," and though
their length is not great, the number of books comprised under that
name is large. "Solomon" usually meant the book of Proverbs, although it could also mean Song of Songs. The phrase "the Prophet"

was also used sometimes to indicate a definite prophetic book of the Old Testament, usually with enough of the original passage to establish identification of it. Of course, it must be remembered that Milton was writing for an age much more familiar than our own with the Bible, and these seemingly inadequate and fragmentary hints were doubtless more than enough to enable Milton's contemporaries to identify the passages on which he was drawing. Needless to say, I have included all actual quotations of this nature here.

A principle seems to have been observed in the use of Scripture in the manner just described. Always artful in the adaptation of written material to his reading public, perhaps Milton was never more so than in the way in which he fitted Biblical passages into his various prose works. When he was writing for and addressing himself to the general reader, he seemed to avoid always the precise citation and actual chapter and verse reference, as when in *Of Reformation*, he gave no precise references at all. In the second chapter of the *Reason of Church Government* occur other generalized references without specific chapter and verse citation, although it is apparent that they are almost exact quotations. This particular practice is observable almost everywhere in Milton's prose, but more noticeably in the prose written for the general reader. Its opposite, specific citation with accompanying quotation, is equally noticeable in the more technical works, reaching its fitting climax in the highly specialized treatise, the *de doctrina*. In this work, practically every reference to the Bible is presented with chapter and verse and actual quotation.

3. The *Quotations, In English, Agreeing with a Definite Text*

Of all the actual quotations in Milton's English prose works, the overwhelming majority of those which agree with any recognized English version at all, agree with the Authorized Version. Of course, one must employ an edition of this version contemporary with Milton. When this is done, the agreement of the majority of his quotations in English with the Authorized Version is markedly apparent.[6]

A list of the English Bibles connected with Milton indicates that his own family Bibles were copies of the Authorized Version. The Genevan Version, sometimes connected with him, has mistakenly

---

[6] For collation of Milton's English Biblical quotations, I have used a Barker Bible, 1611, 1612, 1613, 1617; and a Norton and Bill, 1619.

been suggested as a source for his Biblical quotations. This mistake arose from the fact that a Bible very intimately connected with him was actually a copy of the Genevan Version. But this Bible belonged to his third wife, Elizabeth Minshull. Baxter listed the English Bibles connected with Milton as follows:

1. Breeches Bible (Genevan Version, 1560.)

A copy of this edition was sold a number of times about a generation ago as a copy of a Bible belonging to the poet. But the signature therein has been declared a forgery. Dr. Aldis Wright was of the opinion that this Bible belonged to Major John Milton of the City of London Trained Bands. This Bible attracted considerable interest at the time of its last appearance in the book-market, cf. *London Daily News*, 12 Nov. 1907; and *Notes and Queries*, 10:ix:27. In the *Times* of 13 Dec. 1907 appeared a statement that the description of the Bible as a "Breeches" Bible was incorrect. If this is true, as seems probable, the Bible in question is that next described.

2. Genevan Version, London, (Christopher Barker) 1588, 4to.

This is a black-letter quarto. The poet's signature is written (John Milton ffeb. 24: 1654) on a piece of rough paper 3 1/2 inches by 1 1/2 inches pasted inside the front cover. Underneath this are written "William Minshull, Nantwich" (said to be a relation of Milton's third wife,) and "Thos. Minshull, Middlewich." On the third fly-leaf are "Mary Mathews, Middlewich," and "Eliz. Mingham;" on the second fly-leaf, "J. Mathews." At the top of the title of the New Testament is the signature "Elizabeth Milton, 1664" (two years after Elizabeth Minshull married Milton as his third wife.) On the last leaf (imprint) are the names of "L. Mathews," "Wm. Minshull," and "Eliz. Mingam 1730." On the fly-leaves at the end are "Elizabeth Minshull" and the following note

> Dec ye 27 1714 I gave this Book to my mother,
> the widow Matthews, but if she dyes before me,
> I desire that it should be Retorn to me againe.
> Wm. Mathews.

There are two other signatures of the Mathews family and a pedigree of several of them. Milton married Elizabeth Minshull 26 Feb. 1662/63, and after Milton's death in 1674 his widow retired to Nantwich, where her family lived. She died there in 1727. The signature *Elizabeth Minshull* on the fly at the end suggests that the Bible belonged to her before her marriage with Milton and that his signature in 1654 (two years after he became wholly blind) must have been cut out of some document and inserted. The volume in any case has an interesting connection with Milton, but was not his own.

3. British Museum Bible, London, Printed by R. Barker, 1612, small quarto. This is a copy of the first quarto edition of the Authorized Version printed in Roman letter. The entries in this Bible were published in facsimile with other autographs and documents, by order of the trustees of the British Museum on the occasion of the Milton Tercentenary.

4. Authorized Version, London, (? Robert Barker,) 1613, small quarto. A copy of this edition with alleged autograph was formerly the property of George Offor (*cf. Notes and Queries* 2:xii:233.) This is probably the next to be described.

5. Authorized Version, London, (Robert Barker,) 1614, small quarto. A copy with the autograph of John Milton on the back of the title-page of the New Testament was in the possession of George Offor, *cf.* Sotheby's *Ramblings*, 1861, pp. 128–29. This copy was destroyed by fire while at Sotheby's sale in 1865.

6. Bible seen by Dr. Birch, 1749–50 who described it as octavo, printed by Young in 1636 (Hunter, *Gleanings*, 1850, p. 54.) There is no known edition by Young in 1636.

7. Bible mentioned by Thomas Kerslake in *Athenaeum*, 5 Jan. 1884. There is no similarity between the signature appearing in this Bible and any other Milton signatures. This is worthless as a Milton Bible.[7]

Critical examination of Baxter's listing shows that Bible number seven is worthless; number one is identical with number two, and number five with number four, a book destroyed by fire; which leaves but two Bibles that can be connected with Milton. These are his own family Bible, now in the British Museum (number three), and the Bible of his third wife (number two). Number six, seen by Birch, may still be in existence, but its whereabouts is unknown. Thus the only Bible extant which can be directly connected with Milton and which he apparently used for a long period of time was a copy of the Authorized Version. This substantiates the evidence of his English Biblical quotations which points toward his almost constant use of the Authorized Version as his regularly employed English Version of Scripture.

As would be expected, Milton's few English quotations from the Apocrypha are from that of the Authorized Version. His English works contain but two actual quotations from the Apocrypha, and these completely agree with the reading of the King James Version.[8]

[7] Baxter, Wynn E., *Notes and Queries*, (1911) 11: iii: 109 *ff*.
[8] Ecclesiasticus 13: 16, *Doctrine and Discipline of Divorce*, Mitford, *Works*, vol. IV: 48; and Ecclesiasticus 37: 27, *ibid.* p. 49.

Because of the fact that in Milton's day the Apocrypha invariably accompanied the Scriptures, he would, if he used the Authorized Version, almost inevitably have used also the Apocrypha in that Version.

4. *Quotations Differing from Any Recognized Text*

Many Biblical passages as Milton presented them differ in their reading from the form in which they are to be found in the Authorized Version. It should be expressly stated, before examining these changes in detail, that such deviations from the text of the Authorized Version are actual changes in its readings, and are never merely agreements with some other English version of Scripture. That is, they represent changes which Milton himself made in the reading of the English text.

Nature of the Changes in Those Quotations which do not Agree with the Authorized Version

It is possible to classify the changes Milton made in his English quotations from Scripture in a somewhat systematic fashion. With reference to each other, these changes fall into different groups, each group containing quotations which have been changed for the same discernible reason.

a. Clipping or Shortened Quotations

One such group, and the first to be discussed here, is made up of quotations of Biblical passages that Milton tended to "clip" in order, apparently, to make them more brief and pointed as he employed them. One of the most striking and typical examples of this 'clipping' is to be found in the following:

Doctrine and Discipline of Divorce, vol. IV:38, "2 Cor. 6:(14.) Mis -yoke not together with infidels"

The reading of the Authorized Version (1612) for this is

Be ye not vnequally yoked together with vnbeleeuers.

Other instances of the same nature follow, some equally striking and others very slight, but all representing a shortening or 'clipping' of the original Biblical texts:

ibid. p. 73, "Wilt thou destroy the righteous with the wicked? That be far from thee; shall not the judge of the earth do right?" (Gen. 18:23,25.)

A. V. "Wilt thou also destroy the righteous with the wicked? . . . . . That be farre from thee . . . . . shal not the Iudge of all the earth doe right?"

Of True Religion, vol. V:413–414, "any Graven Image, but the likeness of any thing in Heaven above, or in the Earth beneath, or in the Water under the Earth, thou shalt not bow down to them nor worship them, for I the Lord thy God am a Jealous God." (Ex. 20:4,5.)

A.V. "any grauen Image, or any likenesse of any thing that is in heauen aboue, or that is in the earth beneath, or that is in the water vnder the earth. Thou shalt not bow downe thy selfe to them, nor serue them: for I the LORD thy God am a iealous God,"

Tetrachordon, vol. IV:215, "after the doings of Egypt ye shall not do." Levit. 18 (:3.)

A.V. "After the doings of the land of Egypt wherein ye dwelt, shall ye not doe:"

Tenure of Kings, ibid. p. 462, "When thou art come into the Land which the Lord thy God giveth thee, and shalt say I will set a King over mee, like as all the Nations about mee." Deut. 17:14.

A.V. "When thou art come vnto the land which the LORD thy God giueth thee, and shalt . . . . say, I will set a king ouer me, like as all the nations that are about me."

ibid. "What portion have we in David, or Inheritance in the son of Jesse? See to thine own House David." (1 Kings 12:16.)

A.V. "What portion haue wee in Dauid? neither haue we inheritance in the son of Iesse: . . . . now see to thine owne house, Dauid."

ibid. p. 463, "Thus saith the Lord yee shall not goe up, nor fight against your brethren, for this thing is from me." 1 Kings 12:24.

A.V. "Thus saith the LORD, Ye shall not goe up, nor fight against your brethren the children of Israel: returne euery man to his house, for this thing is from me."

Reason for Church Government, vol. III:139, "Wo is me my mother, that thou hast born me a man of strife, and contention." (Jeremiah 15:10.)

A.V. "Woe is mee, my mother, that thou hast borne mee a man of strife, and a man of contention to the whole earth:"

Doctrine and Discipline of Divorce, vol. IV:85, "have ye not read that he which made them at the beginning, made them male and female, and said, for this cause shall a man cleave to his wife?" (Matt. 19:4,5.)

A.V. "Haue ye not read, that he which made them at the beginning, made them male and female?   And said, For this cause shal a man leaue father and mother, and shall cleaue to his wife: and they twaine shal be one flesh."

Tetrachordon, p. 184, "and should not I unbind a daughter of Abraham from this bond of Satan?" Luke 13 (:16.)

A.V. "And ought not this woman beeing a daughter of Abraham, whom Satan hath bound, loe these eighteene yeeres, be loosed from this bond on the Sabbath day?"

ibid. p. 147, "The head of the woman is the man: he the image and glory of God, she the glory of the man:" 1 Cor. 11 (:3,7.)

A.V. "the head of the woman is the man, ... he is the image and glory of God: but the woman is the glory of the man."

Treatise of Civil Power, vol. V:307, "and exalting himself above all that is called god, or is worshipd," 2 Thess. 2:4.

A.V. "and exalteth himselfe aboue all that is called God, or that is wor-shipped:"

The changes Milton made in these quotations are slight, and in all tend to shorten the quotations in which they severally occur. Perhaps the most important fact concerning these 'clipped' quo-tations is their actual occurrence, and what is most significant about them is that Milton felt warranted in making these slight changes. For all of them appear in his printed works as *bona fide* quotations from Scripture, in spite of the fact that they were not quoted *verbatim*. The slight nature of their differences from the reading of the Authorized Version is discernible as a shortening only. This makes of them a group that represents the simplest of Milton's changes or deviations from a recognized Scriptural text.

b. The Use of Marginal Readings Occurring in the Authorized Version

Another easily recognizable group of deviations from the text of the Authorized Version is formed by those quotations which dis-play the influence of marginal readings found in that Version. Not many such deviations occur, but there are enough to show a tendency to use them. I cite here a few of the instances I have noted of Mil-ton's use of word or phrase found in the margin of the Authorized Version rather than in the text itself. There are not many of such changes, and the following will be sufficient to indicate their nature:

A Treatise of Civil Power, vol. V:322, "in another place is also written of the Pharises, Luke 7:30. *that they frustrated the councel of God.*"

A.V. "the Pharisees and Lawyers #reiected the counsell of God" with marginal note "#*Or, frustrated.*"

Tenure of Kings, vol. IV:451, "That doe the worke of the Lord negligently," (Jer. 48:10.)

A.V. "that doeth the worke of the LORD #deceitfully," with marginal note, "#*Or, negligently.*"

Another quotation, which shows the influence of the marginal note of the Authorized Version, is one which cannot be fully explained as having been influenced by the marginal reading. But because Milton actually used the word found in the margin, the quotation is included here, with more complete discussion of its deviation from the Authorized text *infra*:

Of Reformation, vol. III:22, "And it shall be that that which is in the bridle shall be holy to the Lord." Zachariah (*sic*) (14:20.)

A.V. "In that day shall there be vpon the #bels of the horses, HOLINES VNTO THE LORD," with marginal note, "#*Or, bridles.*"

It should be noted, however, that Milton's employment of marginal notes and commentaries found in *any* Bible was not constant. He sometimes employed the notes found in the margins of the editions of the Authorized Version, though perhaps he more frequently did not. He may always be suspected of having used the marginal notes and other critical apparatus to be found in any Bible that may be connected with him. But an examination of his actual use of such material indicates that for any particular portion of it the necessity is always present of an actual check of his practice in every possible case. That is, Milton used the material he found appended to the texts of the various Bibles he employed. But he did not invariably and indiscriminately allow such material to affect his textual readings. His use of Biblical critical apparatus was highly selective.

c. Shortenings of Quotations by Changes in Phrasing rather than Omissions

So far in this discussion, with the single exception of the last quotation presented above, none of Milton's quotations that have been presented have exhibited radical deviation from the text of the

Authorized Version or decided change of it. The use of marginal variants has been the nearest approach we have so far noted to marked changes of the text, and these have been supplied from the margins of the Authorized Version itself. Even the 'clippings' were not actual changes, being but omissions of parts of the original, picking up the Authorized text again after an omission.

The next group of Milton's quotations with which I propose to deal, is made up of decided variants from the reading of the text of the Authorized Version. As a group, these quotations constitute a collection for which it is extremely difficult to find a common denominator. Each of them is a quotation which exhibits a slight but distinct change of the reading of the Authorized text or deviation from it. The deviation in each case consists almost wholly of change in phrasing by Milton, very slightly affecting the sense but not the spirit of the Authorized reading. The results of these slight changes are various. Sometimes they appear as semi-paraphrastic, but perhaps more often as a kind of 'clipping.' Milton's true 'clippings' as we have seen, are arrangements that omit part or parts of the Authorized text. Sometimes, a true 'clipping' may, by omission of an integral portion of the original, perceptibly change the meaning of the text. Unlike true 'clipping,' the group of quotations now under discussion is made up of alterations of the text which never completely change its meaning. While sometimes shortening the original, they do so by changing the phrasing of it, not by omission. The result is often an actual shortening, not by omitting part of the original, but by the use of briefer phrasing. But the actual quotations themselves, or some of them, are much more valuable indications of what Milton was doing than any description of them. A few examples of this type of change are sufficient to indicate its nature:

Doctrine and Discipline of Divorce, vol. IV:47, "Thou shalt not sowe thy vineyard with divers seeds, lest thou defile both." Deut. 22 (: 9.)

A.V. "Thou shalt not sowe thy vineyard with diuers seeds: lest the fruit of thy seed which thou hast sowen, and the fruit of thy vineyard be defiled."

ibid. p. 64, "To blot out the memory of sin the Amalekite from under heav'n, not to forget it." Deut. 25 (:19.)

A.V. "thou shalt blot out the remembrance of Amalek from vnder heauen: thou shalt not forget it."

Reason of Church Government, vol. III: 148, "She crieth without, she uttereth her voice in the streets, in the top of high places, in the chief concours, and the openings of the Gates." (Prov. 1:20,21.)

A.V. "Wisedome crieth without, shee vttereth her voice in the streets: Shee cryeth in the chiefe place of concourse, in the openings of the gates:"

Doctrine and Discipline of Divorce, vol. IV:100, "a bad wife is to her husband, as rott'nnesse to his bones," (Prov. 12:4.)

A.V. "she that maketh ashamed, is as rottennesse in his bones."

ibid. p. 112, "track of an Eagle in the aire, or the way of a ship in the Sea:" Pro. 30:19,20.

A.V. "The way of an Eagle in the ayre; . . . . the way of a ship in the midst of the sea,"

ibid. p. 29, "love is stronger then death, many waters cannot quench it, neither can the floods drown it." (Cant. 8:6,7.)

A.V. "loue is strong as death, ... Many waters cannot quench loue, neither can the floods drowne it:"

Colasterion, ibid. p. 359, "when the Blackamore changes his colour, or the Leopard his spots." Ier. 13:23.

A.V. "Can the Ethiopian change his skin? or the leopard his spots?"

Reason of Church Government, vol. III:140, "all his familiar friends watcht for his halting" Ieremiah (20:10.)

A.V. "all my familiars watched for my halting,"

Observations on Articles of Peace, vol. IV:572, "be asham'd every one of his lying Vision, as speak Lies in the name of the Lord," Zech. 13:3, 4.

A.V. "bee ashamed euery one of his vision, ... thou speakest lies in the Name of the LORD:"

This group of quotations is of importance chiefly because of the evidence it affords of Milton's attitude toward the text of Scripture as represented by the Authorized Version. Because of the changes appearing in these quotations, and more particularly because of the casual manner in which he changed them, they indicate, as a group and separately, his feeling of freedom toward the Authorized text of Scripture. The changes he made in these quotations, slight but distinctive as they are, point toward his entire willingness to deviate from the Authorized text when quoting the Bible in English.

In order to discover the significance of this willingness to deviate from the Authorized text, it is necessary to examine another and perhaps the most important group of Milton's quotations from Scripture which agree with no recognized text.

c. *Quotations which Represent Milton's Own Version of Scripture*

The group of quotations which has just been discussed is separated from the group I am now about to discuss by a single consideration. In the group previously discussed, the slight changes that appear are of a nature which cannot be explained by assuming an attempt at a closer approximation by Milton of the original Greek or Hebrew respectively of the New or Old Testaments. That is, the changes themselves in the group of quotations discussed above do not arise from the nature of the originals, but appear to have been mere capricious variations of phrasing by Milton for no other apparent reason than that he preferred them so.

There are, however, a number of quotations in Milton's English prose works which are chiefly explicable in their variations from the Authorized text as his own renderings or translations of the original Greek or Hebrew. Milton cited the authority of various recognized translators for some of them. But for the most part, these variants clearly represent his own translations of the passages he cited and quoted. Some of them differ but little, indeed, almost imperceptibly, from the reading of the Authorized text, while others are widely divergent. But each quotation in this class of variants can be definitely explained on the basis of the original Hebrew or Greek that lies back of it.

As each of these quotations can be explained by special considerations applicable to that quotation alone, it will be necessary to consider each separately. I include here and cite all variants, which in my opinion belong to this classification, in order to give some idea of their nature and amount.

I am sure that there is ample opportunity for difference of opinion in connection with the classification of these and other variant quotations. For instance, another person might hold that what I have seen fit to call "Milton's Use of Marginal Variants" might well be included in this discussion of his actual variations from a recognized text, due to his own translations of the originals. Also, it would be entirely possible to include here many of the variants noted in the previous group. But to me there does not appear sufficient warrant for treating those quotations as if they were Milton's own translations. I have not been able to discover adequate reasons for believing that they were. But for the passages that follow, the reasons are sufficiently apparent to me to warrant the assertion that these variants represent his own variation from a recognized version. For lack of a better name, Milton's variation in this respect may be termed his own version of Scripture.

Let me hasten to add that none of the variants appearing in this section of the discussion is in agreement with any other standard version or translation of Scripture than the Authorized. There are a few cases, not included in this section of course, in which Milton himself stated that he had made a change from the Authorized text because of the reading of some other version. But his readings for the group of variants now under discussion are never those of another version. He sometimes incorporated a word or idea from another translator, then gave his own version for the whole quotation. But this will be more apparent as the various quotations in this group are severally discussed.

Before turning to that discussion, I wish to point out the importance of this group of quotations to an understanding of Milton's deviations from recognized Scriptural texts. This group, as already stated, is made up of quotations representing his own version of the Scriptural text, or his own translation of the original Hebrew or Greek. This provides the key to the reason for all his deviations throughout his works, wherever occur his uses of variations from recognized textual readings. Because of his knowledge of the original Hebrew and Greek of the Bible, Milton felt free to make any change he saw fit in the readings of various versions. It was the Bible in its originals that was important to him, not the versions. This attitude toward the text of Scripture, the assumption that he was as capable as any other translator to deal with the originals, accounts fully for Milton's willingness to deviate from all recognized versions whenever he found occasion to do so.

Turning now to the examination of those quotations which clearly show Milton's use of his own version of Scripture, the first to engage attention is the following:

Doctrine and Discipline of Divorce, vol. IV:23, "It is not good that man should be alone;" (Gen. 2:18.)

A.V. "It is not good that the man should be alone:"

Milton's omission of the article before the word *man* was apparently
a trivial omission and nothing more. But the same quotation was
repeated in the *Tetrachordon*, *ibid.* p. 144, and again without the
article. Though the point may be small, it is explicable. The orginal
reading for this particular verse in the Hebrew was the real basis for
Milton's slight change from the Authorized text. The Hebrew reads:

לא טוב היות האדם לבדו

The word האדם (*the-man*) occurs, it is true, with the definite article
הּ (*the*) in the Hebrew. But it likewise occurred in the first chapter
of Genesis, the twenty-seventh verse, in the expression

ויברא אלהים את האדם בצלמו

(and-created God the-man in-image-his)

In this verse in the first Chapter of Genesis, the Authorized text
treated this word האדם, also with the article, as a generic term, and
translated the phrase as *so God created man in his own image*. Milton
apparently preferred to consider the expression לא טוב היות האדם לבדו
in Genesis 2:18 as also referring to generic *man* rather than to an
individual.

Another such slight variation from the Authorized text occurs:

Eikonoklastes, vol. III:527, "To bind thir Kings in chaines, and thir Nobles
with links of Iron," (Psalms 149:8.)

A.V. "To bind their Kings with chaines: and their Nobles with fetters
of yron."

Milton's was a slightly different translation of the Hebrew phrase
בכבלי ברזל (*fetters of iron*.) His "in chaines" for the expression "with
chaines" of the Authorized text is of slight consequence, both ade-
quately translating the Hebrew בכבלי (*in-chains*, or *with-chains*.)

Another of Milton's preferential translations of the Hebrew occurs:

Ready and Easy Way, vol. V:430, "Go to the Ant, ... which having no
Prince, Ruler, or Lord, etc." (Prov. 6:6–8.)

A.V. "Go to the Ant, ... Which hauing no guide, ouerseer, or ruler,"

Just why Milton chose the words *Prince, Ruler, or Lord*, for the
Hebrew קצין שטר ומשל is undeterminable, but choose them he did,
with the resulting variation from the Authorized text. The words
permit of the meanings he gave them, but they also permit of others,
including those found in the standard text.

Another distinctly preferred translation of a Hebrew word, this time slightly nearer the true meaning of the Hebrew than the word used in the Authorized text occurs:

Tetrachordon, vol. IV:155, "I was dayly his delight, playing alwayes before him." (Prov. 8:30.)

A.V. "I was dayly his delight, reioycing alwayes before him."

The same substitution of the word *play* for the Authorized text's *rejoice* occurs later, in *Paradise Lost*.[9] The Hebrew word שחק means to *play* or *sport*. Milton's meaning is, perhaps, one nearer to certain other uses of the Hebrew word than is that of the Authorized text.

A dual change from the Authorized reading occurs in the following:

Of Prelatical Episcopacy, vol. III:80, "My Son, honour God & the King;" (Prov. 24:21.)

A.V. "My sonne, feare thou the LORD, and the King:"

The first change from the Authorized Version here is the use of *honour* instead of *fear* for the Hebrew imperative ירא in the expression ירא את יהוה בני ומלך (*fear* or *honour Yahweh my son, and* [the] *king.*) The other is the substitution of the word *God* for *Lord*, each of these representing the Hebrew יהוה (*Yahweh.*) The same quotation occurs, with the remainder of the verse added, in

Brief Notes on a Sermon, vol. V. 391, "My Son, fear God and the King, and meddle not with them that be Seditious, or desirous of change." Prov. 24:21.

A.V. "My sonne, feare thou the LORD, and the King: and meddle not with them that are giuen to change."

This time, Milton has followed the Authorized text for the first verb, but again translated יהוה as *God*. For the remainder of the verse, he has translated the Hebrew עם שונים אל תתערב (*with changers not thou-meddle*) in a manner suggestive of both the Authorized and Genevan Versions. The Genevan version used the word *seditious*, while the Authorized, as quoted above, used *change*. But Milton's finished reading was like neither version, but peculiar to himself.

Likewise, he twice translated another verse from Proverbs, both times differing from the Authorized translation, and both times translating into the same words. The first occasion was:

---

[9] Book VII : 10.

Doctrine and Discipline of Divorce, vol. IV:81, "a hated woman (for so the Hebrew word signifies, rather then odious though it all come to one) that a hated woman when she is married, is a thing that the earth cannot bear." Prov. 30:21,23.

A.V. "For three things the earth is disquieted, and for foure which it cannot beare: For an odious woman when shee is married,"

He expressed this again in

Tetrachordon, ibid. p. 183, "a hated or a hatefull woman, when shee is married, is a thing for which the earth is disquieted and cannot bear it;"

The distortion of the Biblical order of phrasing is of no consequence here, but Milton's quibbling over the translation of the Hebrew word שנואה is interesting. His translation of the word as *hated* was as good as that of the Authorized Version, though perhaps no better.

Another quotation shows considerable deviation from the standard text in the translation of the following passage:

Of Reformation, vol. III:22, "And it shall be that that which is in the bridle shall be holy to the Lord." Zachariah (*sic*) (14:20.)

A.V. "in that day shall there be vpon the #bels of the horses, HOLINES VNTO THE LORD," #margin, "*Or, bridles.*"

Milton's word *bridle* came, as we have seen, clearly enough from the margin of the Authorized Version. But his reading of the whole passage differed noticeably. He attempted a closer translation of the Hebrew ביום ההוא יהיה על מצלות הסוס קדש ליהוה. Literally translated, this is *in the* (or *that*) *day that which on bells* (of) *the horse holy to Yahweh*. The meaning of this verse is slightly uncertain, but there is nothing uncertain about Milton's closer approximation to the Hebrew than that secured by the Authorized Version.

A curious instance, with confirmatory repetitions, in which Milton was certain that he had discovered a warrant in the original Hebrew for a desired meaning of a Biblical text, is seen in the following:

Doctrine and Discipline of Divorce, vol. IV:34, "Yea God himself commands in his Law more then once, and by his Prophet Malachy, as Calvin and the best translations read, that *he who hates let him divorce;*" Mal. 2:16.

A.V. "he (God) hateth putting away:" the margin reads *if hee hate her, put her away*.

This same verse was used to his own advantage in two others of the Divorce tracts. In each case, Milton followed the translation he had shown preference for above. The second time he used it in:

Judgment of Martin Bucer, vol. IV:319, "Take heed to your spirit, and let none deal injuriously against the wife of his youth. If he hate, let him put away, saith the Lord God of Israel. And he shall hide thy violence with his garment,"

A.V. "take heed to your spirit, and let none deale treacherously against the wife of his youth. For the LORD the God of Israel saith, that he hateth putting away: for one couereth violence with his garment,"

There is no discussion of this verse from Malachi in the *Judgment of Martin Bucer*, and Milton had nothing to say here of different interpretations of the passage. Nevertheless, Milton's full treatment of these verses is one of the most illuminating examples we have of the operation of his complete Biblical equipment. He referred to and quoted the verse again in:

Tetrachordon, vol. IV:176, "Let him who hateth put away saith the Lord God of Israel."

In connection with his employment of the verse here, he exhibited all, or at least a great many of the critical means he had at his command. In his discussion of this in the *Tetrachordon*, he displayed considerable skill in dealing with the question of a proper reading for the Hebrew original. He discussed various translations and commentaries upon the text, and also mentioned the nature of the Hebrew reading itself. But he produced a reading which was peculiarly his own.

As a matter of fact, and Milton noted this, the text of this passage in the original is highly corrupt. The Hebrew reads:

כי שנא שלח אמר יהוה אלהי ישראל

An adequate and satisfactory translation of this is impossible. The translators Milton mentioned have, indeed, disagreed upon the interpretation of the passage. The Authorized Version, with the marginal note, presented two translations, which are quite different from one another. Milton emphatically insisted that what was put in the margin was the true translation. But he supported his point at some length, supplying other authorities.[10] He invoked the translation of

___

[10] *Tetrachordon*, After having cited and quoted Mal. 2: 16, Milton continued, "Although this place also hath bin tamper'd with, as if it were to be thus render'd, *The Lord God saith, that hee hateth putting away*. But this new interpretation rests only in the autority of Junius; for neither Calvin, nor Vatablus himself, nor any other known Divine so interpreted before. And they of best note who have translated the Scripture since, and Diodati for one, follow not his reading. And perhaps they

Calvin but did not quote it.[11] He mentioned also Junius's translation, or the translation found in the Bible which Junius helped edit.[12] For the reading of the verse which Milton here provided, he had gone directly to the Hebrew, translated it to the best of his ability, and then has sought, by means of the authority of other translators, to support his own translation. He has selected a translation differing from that found in the Authorized Version. The passage over which he was concerned is a passage which cannot be translated without emendation of the original. But Milton's time was not a time that emended Biblical readings. Milton's result is, therefore,

might reject it, if for nothing els, for these two reasons: First, it introduces in a new manner the person of God speaking less Majestic then he is ever wont; When God speaks by his Profet, he ever speaks in the first person; thereby signifying his Majesty and omni-presence. Hee would have said, I hate putting away, saith the Lord; and not sent word by Malachi in a sudden faln stile, The Lord God saith that he hateth putting away: that were a phrase to shrink the glorious omnipresence of God speaking, into a kind of circumscriptive absence. And were as if a Herald in the Atcheivment of a King, should commit the indecorum to set his helmet side-waies and close, not full fac't and open in the posture of direction and command. Wee cannot think therefore that this last Profet would thus in a new fashion absent the person of God from his own words as if he came not along with them. For it would also be wide from the proper scope of this place: hee that reads attentively will soon perceav, that God blames not heer the Jews for putting away thir wives, but for keeping strange Concubines, to the profaning of Juda's holines, and the vexation of thir Hebrew wives, v. 11. and 14. Judah hath maried the daughter of a strange God: And exhorts them rather to put thir wives away whom they hate, as the Law permitted, then to keep them under such affronts. And it is receiv'd that this Profet livd in those times of Ezra and Nehemiah (nay by som is thought to bee Ezra himself) when the people were forc't by these two Worthies to put thir strange wives away. So that what the story of those times, and the plain context of the 11 verse, from whence this rebuke begins, can give us to conjecture of the obscure and curt Ebraisms that follow, this Profet does not forbid putting away, but forbids keeping, and commands putting away according to Gods Law, which is the plainest interpreter both of what God will, and what he can best suffer. Thus much evinces that God there commanded divorce by Malachi, and this confirmes that he commands it also heer by Moses."

[11] "Si odio habeas (quisquis odio habet) dimittet (uxorem), dicit Iehova Deus Israel." *Corpus Reformatorum*, Brunsvigae, 1890, vol. 72. *Ioannis Calvini Opera Exegetica et Homiletica*, ediderunt Eduardus Reuss et Alfredus Erichson, vol. XXII, p. 455.

[12] Immanuel Tremellius, et Franciscus Junius, *Biblia Sacra*, Hanoviae, MDXCVI. *Sibi odio esse dimissionem ait Jehova Deus Jisraelis*, with the following note in the margin, "occupatio defensionis Judaeorum: atqui dimittetur uxor ex lege, Deut. 24. ut adducitur Matth. 5. 31. Respondet Propheta, hoc vero odit Deus, neque passurus est ut legem suam adhibeatis tamquam pallium ad tegendam & defendendam injuriam quamveritati ipsius facitis & vestris ipsorum uxoribus: neque enim Deus dimissionem probavit, sed odio habet; ut ipsa legis verba ostendunt Deut. 24. 4."

supported by as many authorities as he could muster. We are not particularly interested in his translation, but his procedure is significant.

Peculiarities of Milton's Quotation of New Testament Texts

Although we are not primarily interested here in Milton's deviations from the Authorized text of the New Testament, in a survey of his attitude toward the text of Scripture these must be included. I therefore insert here his most striking deviations from the standard English text of the New Textament.

As for the Old Testament, Milton frequently quoted passages from the New which contained his own translations of words and phrases from the Greek original. Of course these words and phrases of his selection differ from the reading of the Authorized or any other English version. A list of these variations, together with the Authorized readings, and with the differences italicized, follows:

Doctrine and Discipline of Divorce, vol. IV:2, "Every Scribe instructed to the Kingdome of Heav'n, is like *the Maister of a house* which bringeth out of his *treasury* things new and old." Matth. 13:52.

A.V. "euery Scribe which is instructed vnto the kingdome of heauen, is like vnto *a man that is an housholder*, which bringeth forth out of his *treasure* things new and old."

Of Civil Power, vol. V: 334, "*A heathen or* a publican," Mat. 18:17.

A.V. "*an heathen man, and* a Publicane."

Tenure of Kings, vol. IV: 470, "The Princes of the Gentiles excercise *Lordship* over them," Matt. 20:25.

A.V. "the princes of the Gentiles exercise *dominion* ouer them,"

Of Civil Power, vol. V:310, "there is *none who doth* a *powerfull work* in my name, and can *likely* speak evil of me." Marc. 9:39.

A.V. "there is *no man, which shall doe a miracle* in my Name, that can *lightly* speake euill of me." (I suspect Milton's "likely" of being a misprint only of the A.V. "lightly.")

Doctrine and Discipline of Divorce, vol. IV:83, "*Therefore* shall a man cleave to his wife, and they shall be one flesh:" Mark 10:7,8.

A.V. "*For this cause* shall a man . . . . cleaue to his wife, And they *twaine* shal be one flesh:"

Tetrachordon, ibid. p. 246, "They were *amaz'd then* out of measure," Mark 10:26.

A.V. "they were *astonished* out of measure,"

Tenure of Kings, ibid. p. 470, "They *that seem* to rule . . . . but *yee shall not be so,* but *the greatest* among you shall be your *Servant."* Matt. 20:25. Mark 10:42,43.

A.V. "they *which are accompted to rule* ouer the Gentiles . . . . But *so shall it not be among you:* but *whosoeuer of you will be great* among you, shall be your *minister:"*

Tetrachordon, ibid. p. 47, 245, "hee who had no sword *should sell* his garment and buy one:" Luke 22:36.

A.V. "he that hath no sword, *let him sell* his garment, and buy one."

Of Civil Power, vol. V:311, "certain of the *heresie* of the Pharises which beleevd," Acts 15:5.

A.V. "certaine of the *sect* of the Pharisees which beleeued"

ibid. "after the *exactest heresie* of our religion I livd a Pharise." Acts 26:5.

A.V. "after the *most straitest sect* of our religion, I liued a Pharisee."

Doctrine and Discipline of Divorce, vol. IV:72, "the *Law* were ordain'd unto life," Rom. 7:10.

A.V. "the *commandement* which was ordeined to life,"

ibid. "the *Command* is holy, and just, and good," Romans 7:12.

A.V. "the *Commandement* holy, and iust and good."

ibid. p. 63, "a *revenge* to execute wrath upon him that doth evil." Romans 13:4.

A.V. "A *reuenger* to execute wrath vpon him that doth euill."

Of Civil Power, vol. V: 308, "who art thou that judgest *the servant of another?* to his own *Lord* he standeth or falleth: *but he shall stand;* for God is able to make him stand." Romans 14:4.

A.V. "Who art thou that iudgest *another mans seruant?* to his owne *master* hee standeth or falleth. *Yea he shall be holden vp:* for God is able to make him stand."

ibid. p. 307, "*the spiritual man* judgeth all things, *but* he himself is judgd of no man." 1 Cor. 2:15.

A.V. "*hee that is spirituall* iudgeth all things, *yet* hee himselfe is iudged of no man."

Doctrine and Discipline of Divorce, vol. IV:44, "If *a* brother have an *unbeleeving* wife, and she *joyn in consent* to dwell with him" 1 Cor. 7:12.

A.V. "If *any* brother hath a wife *that beleeueth not,* and she *be pleased* to dwell with him,"

There are other variants from the Authorized text of the New Testament similar to those quoted above, but too slight to require quoting in full. In examining these various passages, it becomes apparent that Milton in these cases actually furnished his own translation of the original. In order to do this, he necessarily displayed a complete willingness to make such changes in the reading of the Authorized Version as he saw fit. The Authorized Version was not a form of the Bible which he held to be either sacred or unalterable; it represented for him a convenient form of Scripture on which to depend in English. But he regularly resorted to the practice of changing the reading of this version by furnishing his own translations throughout the prose works of all periods of his life. It was, therefore, a common practice for him.

It is also evident, especially on the basis of the discussion in the *Tetrachordon* of Malachi 2:16, that he felt himself perfectly competent to discuss and pass on textual readings. Such confidence in his own powers was amply warranted, as his own readings for such passages, resting upon the originals, are sound translations. They testify to his possession of considerable knowledge of and training in the use of Hebrew and Greek. Certainly every sort of variation with which we have dealt, adds its bit of evidence to Milton's thorough, accurate, and familiar knowledge of both Old and New Testaments in their original tongues.

d. Biblical Material Fitted to Milton's Context

There remains one other group of Milton's English quotations from Scripture to be considered. This group is made up of those quotations that he fitted into the context of his writing, often in such a way that they became parts of his own sentences. This procedure was a common practice with him, as with all others who quote Scripture to any great extent. But in Milton's case, this kind of garbled quotation is peculiar to the extent that it exhibits the characteristics of his other uses of Biblical quotations. That is, even when he fitted Biblical passages into his own context, he often did so on the basis of changing them in accordance with the reading of the originals. The result is a group of quotations which contains a great deal of information concerning Milton's attitude toward Scripture and use of it. I shall do no more here than list the more important variants from a standard English text arising from adaptation to Milton's context. But those presented here together with the minor and less important variations of this same nature might well be examined in the same or in a similar way to that in which we have

already examined his other variant quotations. Some of these con-
textual variants are most interesting. Instances of Milton's adaptation of the text of Scripture to his own composition abound. Some
of the more notable of such instances follow:

Tenure of Kings, vol. IV:462, "Therfore David first made a Covnant
with the Elders of Israel, and so was by them anointed King," 2 Sam. 5:3.
1 Chron. 11.

A.V. "So all the Elders of Israel came to the King to Hebron, and King
Dauid made a league with them in Hebron before the LORD: and they
anointed Dauid King ouer Israel."

ibid. "And Jehoiada the Priest making Jehoash King, made a Cov'nant
between him and the People," 2 Kings 11:17.

A.V. "And Iehoiada made a couenant betweene the LORD and the king,
and the people, that they should bee the LORDS people; betweene the king
also and the people."

Eikonoklastes, vol. III:529, "But might call to mind, that the Scripture
speakes of those also, who when God slew them, then sought him; yet did
but flatter him with thir mouth, and ly'd to him with thir tongues; for
thir heart was not right with him." (Psalms 78:34.)

A.V. "When he slew them, then they sought him: . . . . they did flatter
him with their mouth: and they lyed vnto him with their tongues. For
their heart was not right with him:"

Tenure of Kings, vol. IV:453, "their mercies, wee read are cruelties"
Prov. 12:10.

A.V. "but the tender mercies of the wicked are cruell."

Articles of Peace, vol. IV:551, "The Spirit of God by Solomon tells us,
Prov. 30:21. That a Servant to reign, is one of the four things for which
the Earth is disquieted, and which it cannot bear:"

A.V. "For three things the earth is disquieted, and for foure which it
cannot beare: For a seruant when hee reigneth"

Doctrine and Discipline of Divorce, ibid. p. 100, "Who so hideth her hideth
the wind, and one of the foure mischiefs that the earth cannot bear."
(Prov. 27:16 and 30:21.)

A.V."Whosoeuer hideth her, hideth the wind" . . . "for foure which it cannot
beare."

Articles of Peace, ibid. p. 551, "We wonder nothing that the Earth is disquieted for these things; but we wonder greatly, if the Earth can bear
them. And albeit the Lord so permit, that Folly be set in great Dignity,
and they which sit in low place; That Servants ride upon Horses, and
Princes walk as Servants upon the Earth," Eccles. 10. ver. 6, 7.

A.V. "Folly is set in great dignity; and the rich sit in low place. I have seene seruants vpon horses, and princes walking as seruants vpon the earth."

Apology, vol. III:307, "No marvell if the people turne beasts, when their Teachers themselves as Isaiah calls them, *Are dumbe and greedy dogs that can never have anough, ignorant, blind, and cannot understand, who while they all look their own way every one for his gaine from his quarter,*" (Isaiah 56:10–11.)

A.V. "His watchmen are blinde: they are all ignorant, they are al dumbe dogs, they cannot barke; sleeping, lying downe, louing to slumber. Yea they are greedy dogs which can neuer haue ynough, and they are shepheards that cannot understand: they all looke to their owne way, euery one for his gaine, from his quarter."

Reason of Church Government, ibid. p. 136. "while establishment of Church matters was neglected, and put off, there was *no peace to him that went out or came in, for I, saith God, had set all men every one against his neighbor.*" (Zech. 8:10.)

A.V. "neither was there any peace to him that went out, or came in, because of the affliction: for I set all men, euery one against his neighbor."

Doctrine and Discipline of Divorce, vol. IV:34, "that will not hearken to St. Paul, 1 Cor. 7. who speaking of mariage and divorce, determines plain enough in generall, that God therein *hath call'd us to peace* and not *to bondage.*"

A.V. "but God hath called vs to peace."

Tetrachordon, ibid. pp. 250–251, "and his manifest conclusion is, not only that *we should not touch,* but that having toucht, *we should come out from among them, and be separat;* with the promise of a blessing thereupon that *God will receave us, will be our father, and we his sons and daughters,* v. 17. 18."

A.V. "Wherefore come out from among them, and be yee separate, saith the Lord, and touch not the vncleane thing, and I will receiue you, And will be a Father vnto you, and ye shall be my sonnes and daughters, saith the Lord Almighty"

Reason of Church Government, vol. III:172, "This is the approved way which the Gospell prescribes, these are the *spirituall weapons of holy censure,* and ministerial *warfare, not carnall, but mighty through God to the pulling downe of strong holds, casting down imaginations, and every high thing that exalteth it selfe against the knowledge of God, and bringing into captivity every thought to the obedience of Christ.*" (2 Cor. 10:4–5.)

A.V. "(For the weapons of our warfare are not carnall, but mighty through God to the pulling downe of strong holds.) Casting downe imaginations, and euery high thing that exalteth it selfe against the knowledge of God, and bringing into captivity euery thought to the obedience of Christ"

Of Prelatical Episcopacy, vol. III:92, "certainly if Christs Apostle have set downe but two, then according to his owne words, though hee himselfe should unsay it, and not onely the Angell of Smyrna, but an Angell from Heaven should beare us downe that there bee three, Saint Paul has doom'd him twise, let him be accurs't." (Gal. 1:8.)

A.V. "But though wee, or an Angel from heauen, preach any other Gospel vnto you, then that which wee haue preached vnto you, let him be accursed."

Tetrachordon, vol. IV:167, "And I again ask, why the Gospel so oft repeats the eating of our Saviours flesh, the drinking of his blood? *That wee are one body with him, the members of his body, flesh of his flesh and bone of his bone."* Ephes. 5 (:30.)

A.V. "For we are members of his body, of his flesh, and of his bones"

Of Reformation, vol. III:4, "which sometimes deceve's wel-meaning men, and beguiles them of their reward, by their voluntary humility, which indeed, is fleshy pride, preferring a foolish Sacrifice, and the rudiments of the world, as Saint Paul to the Colossians explaineth, before a savory obedience to Christs example." (Col. 2:8,18.)

A.V. "after the rudiments of the world, and not after Christ. Let no man beguile you of your reward, in a voluntary humility, and worshipping of Angels, intruding into those things which he hath not seene, vainely puft vp by his fleshy mind."

Doctrine and Discipline of Divorce, vol. IV:82, "it must have an undoubted *end of charity, which may be us'd with a pure heart, a good conscience, and faith unfained,"* (1 Tim. 1:5.)

A.V. "Now the end of the commandement is charity, out of a pure heart, and of a good conscience, and of faith vnfained."

Remonstrant's Defense, vol. III:217, "*Bishops* (saith he) *must not be greedy of filthy lucre, and having food and rayment, let us bee therewith content: but they* (saith hee, meaning more especially in that place *Bishops*) *that will be rich fall into temptation, and a snare, and into many foolish, and hurt-full lusts, which drowne men in destruction, and perdition:* for *the love of money is the root of all evill, which while some coveted after, they have erred from the faith."* (1 Tim. 3:3, and 6:8–10.)

A.V. "A Bishop then must bee" (3:2) "not greedy of filthy lucre" (6:8 no reference to Bishops) "And hauing food and raiment, let vs be therewith content. But they that will bee rich, fall into temptation and a snare, and into many foolish and hurtful lusts, which drowne men in destruction and perdition. For the loue of money is the root of all euill, which while some coueted after, they haue erred from the faith."

Reason of Church Government, ibid. p. 106, "S. Peter, who by what he writes in the 5 Chap. of his first Epistle should seeme to be farre another man then tradition reports him: there he commits to the Presbyters only full authority both of feeding the flock, and Episcopating: and commands that obedience be given to them as to the mighty hand of God, which is his mighty ordinance." (1 Peter 5:1–6.)

A.V. "The Elders which are among you I exhort . . . Feed the flocke of God . . . . being ensamples to the flock. . . . Likewise yee yonger, submit your selues vnto the elder . . . . vnder the mighty hand of God."

Remonstrant's Defense, ibid. p. 244, "and of such Saint John saith, He that bids them God speed, is partaker of their evill deeds." (2 John 11.)

A.V. "For he that biddeth him God speed, is partaker of his euill deedes."

Reason of Church Government, ibid. p. 106, "Arise, said the Angell and measure the Temple of God and the Altar, and them that worship therein." (Rev. 11:1.)

A.V. "and the Angel stood, saying, Rise, and measure the Temple of God, and the Altar, and them that worship therein."

Eikonoklastes, ibid. pp. 527–528, "*These shall hate the great Whore*, and yet *shall give thir Kingdoms to the Beast that carries her; they shall committ Fornication with her*, and yet *shall burn her with fire*, and yet *shall lament the fall of Babylon*, where they fornicated with her. Thus shall they be too and fro, doubtfull and ambiguous in all thir doings, untill at last, *joyning thir Armies with the Beast*, whose power first rais'd them, they shall perish with him by the *King of Kings* against whom they have rebell'd; *and the Foules shall eat thir fleshe.*" (Rev. 17:2)

A.V. "the great Whore . . . with whom the kings of the earth haue committed fornication . . . . and shall giue their power and strength vnto the beast . . . these shall perish . . . . and all the foules were filled with their flesh." (19:21.)

To Remove Hirelings, vol. V:373, "To bow down with his face toward the Earth, and lick up the dust of her Feet." Isaiah 49:23.

A.V. "they shall bow downe to thee with their face toward the earth, and licke vp the dust of thy feete."

Of True Religion, ibid. pp. 414–415, "But with these wiles and fallacies *compassing Sea and Land, like the Pharisees of old, to make one Proselite,* they lead away privily many simple and ignorant Souls, men or women, *and make them twofold more the Children of Hell then themselves,"* Matt.23:15.

A.V. "Woe vnto you Scribes and Pharisees, hypocrites; for ye compasse sea and land to make one Proselyte, and when he is made, ye make him twofold more the child of hel then your selues."

There are many other cases in which Milton wove the Biblical text into his own composition, but those just quoted are the most remarkable of them all. Several of these have been examined earlier on different bases from this one. This is because Milton almost invariably indicated when he was actually quoting, and when he was not, by the use of italics in his printed text.

This concludes the examination of the Biblical quotations in English. We have now seen how Milton's knowledge of the Scriptures in their originals, at once thorough, broad, and accurate, is powerfully supported by his remarkable employment of Biblical quotations throughout his English prose works.

The Quotations in the Latin "pro populo Anglicano Defensio"

Because the Biblical quotations in the *pro populo* are in Latin and hence never taken from the Authorized Version, I deal with them separately from Milton's English quotations. They constitute a group of quotations in Latin, obviously taken mainly from some other source or version. About half of them agree sufficiently with a particular Latin Biblical text to make it clear that this was the text from which they were taken. This text was the Latin Biblical version known as the Junius-Tremellius, published in various forms during the last quarter of the sixteenth century. Milton appears to have followed this text much as he followed the Authorized for his English quotations. When he quoted *verbatim,* it was this text he quoted, and when he varied from it, he was not using another Latin version, but was disagreeing with this one.

This last statement is true for all but two of his variations from the text of Junius-Tremellius. These are the following:

pro populo, vol. VI:38, "Sedit Salmon, inquis, *super solium Domini et cunctis placuit,* 1 Paralip. 29." (1 Chron. 29:23.)

Junius-Tremellius, 1 Chron. 29:23, "solio Iehovae . . . prosperabatur"

Milton's quotation in this instance did not represent a deviation from the Junius-Tremellius text. This is one of the few instances in all his works of his genuine use of some other Latin text of Scripture than Junius-Tremellius. Indeed, it is one of the rare occasions on which he presented a quotation from some definite version other than the Authorized or the Junius-Tremellius. In this case, the version from which he quoted is easily found, for it was the Vulgate, which reads as follows for this passage:

1 Paralip. 29:23, "super solium Domini et cunctis placuit"

This might constitute a perplexing case of Milton's use of the Vulgate, for he so seldom did use it that it might be said that he never intended to do so. It would have been most unusual had one of the arch-Protestants of seventeenth century England made regular use of the official Roman Catholic Biblical text. But, if the nature of the *pro populo* be remembered, the reason for this quotation from the Vulgate here is easily explained. In this work, Milton answered in their original order the points made by Salmasius. He followed Salmasius through the latter's maze of Biblical quotations, and, at least in this case, used Salmasius's own quotation from the Vulgate rather than a quotation from Junius-Tremellius. Salmasius's whole statement and Biblical quotation were as follows:

"inde est quod solium in quo rex sedet *solium Dei* in Sacra Scriptura dicitur ut Paralipomenon lib. I. cap. xxix. *Seditque Salomon super solium domin in regem pro David patre suo, et cunctis placuit, et paruit illi omnis Israel.*"[1]

One other such agreement with the Vulgate appears in the *pro populo*:

pro populo, ibid. p. 42, "*tibi soli peccavi*" (Ps. 51:6.)

This was a very slight change from Junius-Tremellius's *tibi soli peccaveram.* It might be passed over in silence were it not for the fact that Milton's quotation was exactly that of the Vulgate, and again he was following Salmasius.[14] A check of Salmasius's quotations discloses the fact that the Frenchman used the Vulgate throughout the *defensio regia.* This was natural enough, but we catch a glimpse of Milton's supreme disdain for Catholicism in his refusal, for all but the two just pointed out, to accept Salmasius's Biblical quotations from

---

[13] Cl. Salmasii *Defensio Regia pro Carolo I*, etc. Anno M. DC. LII. p. 58.
[14] *ibid.* p. 59, "a Deo veniam petens, erupit Ps. LI. v. VI. *tibi soli peccavi.*"

the Vulgate. Laboriously, Milton substituted for most, in fact for all but these two of Salmasius's Vulgate quotations, quotations taken for the most part from the Protestant Junius-Tremellius. A curious instance of Milton's insistence that the latter was a better version than the Vulgate occurs in the following:

pro populo, ibid. p. 46, "Deut. 17. supprimis enim veteratorie quod praecedit, *si dixeris, satuam super me regem*"

As a matter of fact, Salmasius quoted the entire text from the Vulgate as follows:

"Diserte enim confutatur his verbis Moysis sole clarioribus, sicut in Deuteronomio XVII. habentur, & mandatum continent de rege creando: *Cum ingressus fueris terram quam Dominus Deus dabit tibi, & possederis eam, habitaverisque in illa, & dixeris, constituam super me regem sicut habent omnes per circuitum nationes, eum constitues quem Dominus Deus elegerit, ex numero fratrum tuorum.*"[15]

This is very nearly identical with the Vulgate:

Deut. 17:14, "Cum ingressus fueris Terram, quam Dominus Deus tuus dabit tibi, et possederis eam, habitauerisque in illa, et dixeris: Constituam super me regem, sicut habent omnes per circuitum nationes: eum constitues, quem Dominus Deus tuus elegerit de numero fratrum tuorum."

But Milton's fragmentary quotation was from Junius-Tremellius. Contrary to what Milton said, nothing from the Vulgate was left out or garbled in Salmasius's quotation. Milton seemed to have felt that he was substituting a better rendering for Salmasius's inferior one. Later in his work, Salmasius quoted a portion of these verses, *ponendo pones super te regem*, and it was to this second quotation that Milton referred, accusing him of having omitted the introductory *et dixeris.*

The Quotations Differing from the Text of Junius-Tremellius

Turning now to the remaining Latin quotations in the *pro populo* which do not agree with the readings found in Junius-Tremellius, I shall present these as they occur.

pro populo, vol. VI:45, "*ad Deum referre*" Exod. 18:19. Tremellius, "tu referas eorum res ad Deum"

p. 29, "*Ut dicto audientes Mosi fuimus, ita erimus tibi, modo ut Deus tecum sit, quemadmodum fuit cum Mose.*" Jos. 1:17.

---

[15] Salmasius, *op. cit.* p. 64.

Tremellius, "Omnino secundum ea quibus auscultavimus Moschi, sic auscultabimus tibi: tantummodo sit Jehova Deus tuus tecum, quemadmodum fuit cum Mosche."

p. 47, "*Non dominabor in vos, neque filius meus in vos dominabitur, sed dominabitur in vos Jehova.*" Judges 8:23.

Tremellius, "non habebo ego dominium in vos, neque filius meus habebit dominum in vos: Iehova habiturus est dominium in vos."

p. 47, "*Non te sed me spreverunt ne regnem super ipsos, secundum illa facta quibus dereliquerunt me et coluerunt Deos alienos:*" 1 Sam. 8:7,8.

Tremellius, "non enim te spreverunt solum, sed me spreverunt; ne regnem super ipsos. Secundum omnia illa facta quae fecerunt a die quo deduxi eos ex Aegypto usque; in hunc diem, quibus dereliquerunt me et coluerunt deos alienos."

p. 35, "*servi vos eritis regi*" 1 Sam. 8:17.

Tremellius, "vos eritis ei servi" (This variant word-order is of no consequence; but the same verse is again quoted p. 37 exactly following Tremellius.)

p. 36, "*Et exclamabitis die illa propter regem vestrum, sed non exaudiet vos Jehovah;*" 1 Sam. 8:18.

Tremellius, "Adeo ut clamaturi sitis die illa propter regem vestrum, quem elegeritis vobis, sed non exaudiet vos Iehova die illa."

p. 47, "*Videte malum verum magnum esse coram Jehova petendo vobis regem.*" 1 Sam. 12:17.

Tremellius, "videte malum vestrum quod fecistis magnum esse in oculis Iehovae, petendo vobis regem"

p. 42, "*reus capitis vir ille qui fecit hoc*" 2 Sam. 12:5.

Tremellius, "reus mortis est vir ille qui fecit hoc"

ibid. "*Tu hoc clam fecisti*" 2 Sam. 12:12.

Tremellius, "Quia tu fecisti clam"

p. 79, "*Quae nobis portio cum Davide? ad tentoria tua Israel: jam ipse videris de domo tua David.*" 1 Kings 12:16.

Tremellius, "quae nobis portio esset cum Davide? utique non est nobis possessio cum filio Iischaji, ad tentoria tua Iisrael, jam vide domui tuae David."

p. 41, "*a facie tua judicium meum prodeat*" Ps. 17:2.

Tremellius, "a facie tua jus meum prodeat"

p. 42, "*tui oculi vident, quae recta sunt, cum exploraveris cor meum*" Ps. 17:2,3.

Tremellius, "oculi tua videant quae recta sunt. Quum exploraveris animum meum"

p. 40, "*vinculis coercerent, inque eos jus scriptum exercerent,*" Ps. 149:8.

Tremellius, "Ad vinciendum reges eorum catenis, et ad exercendum in eos jus scriptum"

p. 29, "*Mandatum regis observa; vel propter juramentum Dei, ne perturbate a facie ejus abito, ne persistito in re mala, nam quicquid volet faciet; Ubi verbum regis, ibi Dominatio, et quis dicat ei quid facis?*" Eccles. 8:1,2.

Tremellius, "Praestitutum meum, praestitutum regis observa; sed pro ratione juramenti Dei. Ne perturbate a facie ejus abito, ne persistito in re mala: nam quicquid volet, facturus esset?"

ibid. "*Verba sapientum submissa potius audienda esse, quam clamorem dominantis inter stolidos.*" Eccles. 9:17.

Tremellius, "Verba sapientium submissorum audienda esse, potius quam clamorem dominantis cum stolidis suis" (verse 19)

p. 82, "*Non is est rex qui possit contra vos quicquam.*" Jer. 38:5.

Tremellius, "nam minime is est Rex qui possit contra vos quicquam"

p. 47, "*Ubi rex tuus, ubinam est? servet te jam in civitatibus tuis. Ubi vindices tui? quoniam dixisti, da mihi regem et proceres: dedi tibi regem in ira mea*" Hos. 13:10,11.

Tremellius, "Ubi est Rex tuus? ubi nam est? is servet ergo te in omnibus civitatibus tuis: ubi vindices tui, de quibus dixeras, da mihi Regem et Principes? Do tibi regem in ira mea"

p. 51, "*a quibus acciperent reges terrae tributa, sive censum, a filiis suis, an ab alienis? respondet ei Petrus, ab alienis; ergo, inquit Christus, liberi sunt filii; sed ne offendamus illos, da iis pro me et pro te.* Matt. 17:25,27.

Beza, "a quibus accipiunt tributa sive censum? a filiis suis, an ab alienis? Dicit ei Petrus, Ab alienis. Ait ei Iesus, Nempe igitur liberi sunt filii. Sed ne offendiculo simus eis . . . . acceptum illum da eis pro me et pro te."

p. 54, "*Scitis,* inquit, *principes gentium in eas dominari, et magnates authoritatem exercere in eas, verum non ita erit inter vos. Sed quicunque volet inter vos magnus fieri, esto vester minister; et quicunque volet inter vos primus esse, esto vester servus?*" (Matt. 20:25–27.)

Beza, "Scitis principes gentium is eas dominari, et magnates potestatem exercere in eas. Verum non ita erit inter vos: sed quicumque voleruit inter vos magnus fieri, esto vester minister: Et quicumque voluerit inter vos primus esse, sit vester servus."

p. 52–53, "*cujus*, inquit, *imago ista est? Caesaris. Reddite ergo Caesari quae sunt Caesaris, quae Dei sunt Deo.*" Matt. 22:20–21.

Beza, "Cuius est imago ista et inscriptio? Dicunt ei, Caesaris: Tunc dicit eis, Reddite ergo quae sunt Caesaris Caesari, et quae sunt Dei Deo."

p. 50–51, "*superbos dissipavit cogitatione cordis ipsorum, detraxit dynastas e thronis, humiles evexii,*" Luke 1:51–52.

Beza, "dissipavit superbos cogitatione cordis ipsorum. Detraxit potentes e thronis, & extulit humiles."

p. 59, "*Tibi dabo potestatem hanc omnem, nam mihi tradita est, et cui volo do illam.*" Luke 4:6.

Beza, "Tibi dabo potestatem hanc universam, et gloriam illorum regnorum: nam mihi tradita est, et cuicumque voluero, do eam."

p. 61, "*Magistratus non sunt timori bonis operibus, sed malis; boni a potestate hac laudem adipiscentur; Magistratus minister est Dei nostro bono datus; non frustra gladium gerit, vindex ad iram ei qui malum facit.*" Rom. 13:3,4.

Beza, "Nam Magistratus non sunt metui bonis operibus, sed malis: Vis autem non metuere potestatem? quod bonum est facito, et laudem ab ipsa obtinebis. Dei enim minister est tuo bono. Quod si feceris quod malum est, metue: non enim frustra gladium gerit: nam Dei minister est, vindex ad iram ei qui quod malum est fecerit."

p. 66, "*orandum, ut vitam tranquillam et quietam transigamus, cum pietate tamen omni et honestate*" 1 Tim. 2:2.

Beza, "ut tranquillam ac quietam vitam degamus cum omni pietate et veneratione."

p. 56, "*subjecti estote omni humanae ordinationi propter Dominum, sive regi ut supereminenti, sive praesidibus, ut qui per eum mittantur, ad ultionem quidem facinorosorum, laudem vero benefacientium; quoniam ita est voluntas Dei.*" 1 Peter 2:13–15.

Beza, "subjecti estote cuivis humanae ordinationi propter Dominum: sive regi, ut supereminenti: Sive praesidibus, ut qui per eum mittantur: tum ad ultionem facinorosorum, tum ad laudem bene agentium. Quoniam ita est voluntas Dei."

p. 59, "*dedit Bestiae Draco potentiam suam, et thronum suum, et potestatem magnam.*" Rev. 13:2.

Beza, "dedit autem ei draco virtutem suam, et thronum suum, et potestatem magnam."

In general, the changes in these Latin quotations from the text of Junius-Tremellius are of the same nature as those previously found in the English quotations differing from the text of the Authorized

Version. Milton regularly employed the Junius-Tremellius text for Latin quotation, but changed it whenever he found it desirable to do so. Some of the changes are distinctly different from the reading of Junius-Tremellius, while others represent "clippings" and the variations noted in connection with the English quotations. The chief importance of the variant quotations cited above is that they actually do differ from the Junius-Tremellius text, from which Milton quoted. Thus, he employed this Latin Scriptural text just as he did the Authorized English Text: it was a convenient translation in that language, but it by no means represented the basic, unalterable text of Scripture. Only the original could claim that peculiar distinction for Milton, and the result is that neither the English nor the Latin version was held by him to be the authentic text of Scripture. That distinction he reserved wholly for the originals.

This investigation of Milton's use of Biblical quotations throughout his works, exclusive of the *de doctrina*, discloses the fact that he possessed a remarkable knowledge and command of the original texts of both the Old and New Testaments. So far as the necessary knowledge of the Old Testament in its original Hebrew is concerned, he has demonstrated by his use of the original that the Hebrew text was, from a very early period in his life, both accessible and well-known to him. He has everywhere exhibited a familiarity with text and critical apparatus possible only through long and constant use of the original Hebrew and of the scholarly tools necessary to its use. The truth of this statement will be even more apparent after an examination of the Biblical quotations of the *de doctrina*, to which we shall now turn our attention.

CHAPTER III.

THE USE OF THE BIBLE IN THE *DE DOCTRINA*

Throughout all his prose works, as we have already seen, Milton quoted Scripture to a marked extent. In the posthumous *de doctrina Christiana*, however, there is an extraordinary amount of such quotation. In the dedication of this work, Milton announced that "De me, libris tantummodo sacris adhaeresco." Every point developed in this theological system was supported by Scriptural reference or quotation. The work itself consists of but little more than a marshalling of Biblical references to support the various theological ideas put forth. Back of it lay a systematic listing of Biblical passages, each under its proper heading, and the whole arranged and compiled in schematic fashion. The complicated assembling and arrangement must have required years of patient collecting and checking of Bible passages, the whole process and the final redaction having been formulated in the mind of their ultimately blind redactor. Milton himself said of the method of the work, "Coepi igitur adolescens cum ad libros utriusque Testamenti lingua sua perlegendos assiduus incumbere, tum Theologorum systemata aliquot breviora sedulo percurrere: ad eorum deinde exemplum, locos communes digerere, ad quos omnia quae ex scripturis haurienda occurrissent, expromenda cum opus esset, referrem."

The result is that the *de doctrina* contains over seven thousand chapter and verse citations of Scripture, more than three-fourths of which include quotations. This document is, therefore, the most important source of information regarding Milton's use of the text of Scripture we possess. Any discussion of his use and knowledge of the Bible must be based on, or at least take full account of his practice in the *de doctrina*, since it is by far the most important single work connected with Milton's knowledge and use of the text of Scripture.

1. The Latin Biblical Version from which Milton Quoted

The first consideration which arises in connection with the Biblical quotations in the *de doctrina* is that of determining from what version and text of the Bible these were quoted, together with an examination of that Biblical version for its peculiarities. There is no problem so far as the version is concerned, but not enough attention has been paid to the particular edition or editions of that version which Milton used. A century or more ago Sumner pointed out that Milton usually employed the Latin Bible that was the work of Tremellius and his collaborator, Francis Junius. In substantiation of this conclusion, Sumner gave at least one minute detail in connection with the *de doctrina*. He pointed out that in one instance, the word *patientia*, in the quotation from Hebrews 4:13, was substituted for the word *patentia*, and said of it, "this might have been supposed an accidental oversight, occasioned by the haste of the writer; but on turning to the Latin of Junius and Tremellius, which Milton generally used in his quotations, it will be found that the same error occurs in the edition printed at Geneva, 1630, but not in that printed at London, 1593. This not only seems to fix the precise edition from which the texts were copied, but, considering that the mistake is such as could hardly fail to be corrected by the most careless transcriber, provided he understood the sentence, affords a strong presumption that the writer possessed a very moderate degree of scholarship."[1]

Very little investigation is necessary in order to confirm Sumner's statement regarding Milton's use of the Junius-Tremellius Bible. Milton mentioned this version as early as his *Divorce* tracts.[2] The same version was likewise mentioned a number of times by name (Junius) in the *de doctrina*, especially when Milton was calling attention to difficulties of translating the Hebrew text.[3] In addition to this, collation of Milton's quotations in the *de doctrina* with a Latin Bible text cannot proceed very far without clear indications that for the most part he intended to quote the Latin of this particular Bible. An extremely large number of the quotations, over ninety out of every hundred, agree precisely or with minor differences with the Latin text of the Junius-Tremellius Latin Bible.[4]

[1] Sumner, Charles, editor, *The Christian Doctrine*, Cambridge, 1825, pp. xv–xvi. For further discussion of this point, *cf. infra* in my present chapter.

[2] vol. IV: 176, *Tetrachordon*.

[3] My references through the remainder of the discussion in this chapter will be to Sumner's beautiful edition of the Latin text of the *de doctrina Christiana*, Cantabrigiae, M. DCCC. XXV. References to Junius-Tremellius occur on pp. 164, 379, and 476 of that edition.

[4] The Junius-Tremellius Bible first appeared between 1575–1579 in sections. That is, as rapidly as Tremellius finished his translations of the various books of the Old Testament, he published each one separately. The first London

II. *Milton's variants from the Junius-Tremellius Text*

In order the better to observe Milton's use of Scripture and quotations therefrom, I have collated every quotation that occurs in the *de doctrina* with a Latin version of the Bible. My collation of these quotations has clearly indicated that for purposes of quotation, Milton almost wholly used the Junius-Tremellius Latin text. But it is what has happened when he did not follow this translation that is of greatest importance here.

When his quotation differs from the text of Tremellius, what has taken place?

---

edition of the complete Bible appeared in 1580. Subsequently the work was frequently printed in two major forms. One of these was, from about 1585 onward, printed as a full folio with a set of marginal notes, which were for the most part written by Tremellius. Notes had also accompanied the text of some of the earlier quartos; but the text itself and the notes of the earlier editions differ from the text and notes of the later editions. Milton probably never quoted from an edition whose text was earlier than that of 1585. Certainly he never quoted from the text of the London edition of 1580. Tremellius translated the Old Testament in its entirety directly from the original Hebrew. He was, as is well-known, a thoroughly competent Semitic scholar, and his translation of the Old Testament became, not only in England, but also on the Continent, almost as standard a Latin translation for the Protestant as the Vulgate had long before become for the Roman Catholic. In addition to this, Tremellius also edited and translated the fragmentary Syriac version of the New Testament which appeared at Paris as early as 1569. Junius's chief contribution to Tremellius's excellent Old Testament was the contribution of an editor. He also acted as editor and collaborator to the edition of the complete Bible. He caused to be added to Tremellius's translation of the Old Testament a standard and complete Latin New Testament. He selected for this purpose the Latin translation of Beza, and the folio editions of the Junius-Tremellius Bible usually carry in parallel columns Tremellius's translation of all those portions of the New Testament which occur in the Syriac, and Beza's translation of the complete Greek. The folio editions contained, therefore, in addition to Tremellius's text and notes of the Old Testament, a complete Latin translation, from the Greek, of the Apochrypha, done by Junius; and two Latin translations of the New Testament, one of these being Beza's Latin translation of his own Greek text of the New Testament, and the other being Tremellius's translation of the fragmentary Syriac. These two New Testament texts were printed in parallel columns on the same pages. Another and more frequent form in which this Bible appeared was in quarto or even smaller size, with Tremellius's Old Testament, with Junius's Apochrypha, with only one text of the New Testament (at first only Tremellius's and, later only Beza's) and without notes. But many editions of both forms, folio and quarto, appeared, the smaller, edition being reprinted more often than the folio. The history of the Junius-Tremellius Bible is important for the student of Milton, and equally important for students of the period beginning about the middle of Elizabeth's reign until the political upheaval of the Interregnum. One catches strange and significant echoes from this important Protestant Biblical version throughout this whole period. *cf.* Baldwin, T. W., (editor) *The Comedy of Errors*, New York, 1928, p. 120 f.

To answer this question will greatly inform us concerning Mil-tons's whole attitude toward Scripture, and will also provide the most adequate basis possible for a determination of how far he felt himself competent to deal with the text of the Old and New Testa-ment originals, in fact with all textual problems.

Among the large number of variants in the *de doctrina* from the Junius-Tremellius text, some may be very readily accounted for and disposed of at once. Thus, Milton's peculiarly free adaptation of Scriptural passages to his context, especially when using a portion of Scripture within his sentences, has already been remarked. This was noted in connection with his other English and Latin prose works, and may also be very often observed in the *de doctrina*. Ex-amples are too numerous to mention in detail, but certain peculiar-ities of these adaptations are of some interest though of no impor-tance. These usually take the form of change in word-order.

Another whole class of inconsequential variants from the Tre-mellius text is made up of changes or peculiarities in Milton's spell-ing. I do not refer to his well-known prejudices of spelling such as appear in his poems, but rather to those changes he made from the spellings found in the Junius-Tremellius text. The most noticeable difference in Milton's spellings from those of Tremellius occur in the proper names. For the most part, it is clearly evident that Milton intended to use for every Biblical proper name, a form that very nearly approximated our modern usage. Most of our modern spell-ings of Biblical proper names are those employed by the Authorized Version, and Milton for the most part followed the spellings of that Version. Tremellius's spellings of proper names are attempts to in-dicate their Hebrew originals. Milton had no intention of following Tremellius's text in this matter. Occasionally, however, some of Tremellius's peculiar spellings crept in, but for every one that got once into Milton's manuscript, a dozen others uses of the same name may be pointed out in which a more common spelling than Tremellius's was used. For instance, Tremellius's spelling was followed in a quotation from 1 Samuel 3:21, page 88, *Schemueli Shilunti*. One needs to look at this a number of times to realize that it represented *Samuel in Shiloh*. But this was not at all Milton's preferred spelling of Samuel. This is best indicated by citing the following quotations in which the name *Samuel* occurs, and where the spelling is never other than our own, although Tremellius's spelling was always

Schemuel: 1 Samuel 7:9 (*sic*) page 532; 10:1, page 472; 10:20, page 433; 13:13, page 502; 15:11, page 422; 19:20, page 515. As I have said, such acceptance of Tremellius's spellings of proper names is very rare. There is a curious example of it in quoting from Isaiah 11:1, page 205, when Milton used *Jischai* (Jesse), the only occurrence of that form of the name I have noted in the manuscript, although there may be others which have escaped me. Their occasional though rare appearance strongly suggests that Milton's statement in the dedication, to the effect that he compiled lists of quotations under appropriate headings, is to be taken literally. That is, a definite method of collecting and arranging Biblical quotations must have been used. Undoubtedly this compilation extended over a long period of years. Vast numbers of the quotations in the *de doctrina* manuscript have been transcribed, perhaps by different amanuenses, from Milton's own copy of some of them. While others must have found their way into the surviving manuscript from copies made by other and earlier amanuenses. For much of the finished work of the manuscript as we now have it, some such procedure must have been the rule, as it seems to me unlikely that all of the quotations in the form transmitted to us could have been first set down as parts of a whole. Rather the collection over a long period of years of quotations under their proper headings would seem a more logical method, and indeed was precisely the method that Milton himself described. In that case, those proper names which follow Tremellius in their spellings would represent quotations copied directly from the Biblical text of Tremellius into the manuscript, and the more modern spellings would represent names which Milton himself had written out earlier, or spellings revised by more frequent copying than that received by those unchanged from Tremellius.

Another change in spelling frequently made by Milton from the spelling found in the Tremellius text is observable in the well-defined intention to substitute the letter *c* for Tremellius's *qu* in certain words. This substitution was, of course, a general tendency of seventeenth century Latin spelling, and not especially peculiar to Milton. But it is noted here because it is a well-defined change in spelling. For such words as Tremellius's *quum* (as a conjunction), *loquutus*, *alloquutus*, and *sequutus*, Milton's intention is quite apparent. His intention was clearly to substitute for the spellings of these words as just noted which *always* occur in Tremellius, the respective spellings *cum*, *locutus*, *allocutus*, and *secutus*.[5] I have noted hundreds of usages of these words in Milton's manuscript, though by no means all that occur. Of course, both forms, *c* and *qu*, occur in the manuscript, there being plenty of unchanged *qu* forms. All the *qu* forms in the manuscript follow *qu* forms in Tremellius. The other *qu* words are not so numerous. *Locutus* changed from Tremellius's *loquutus* occurs in the following quotations, and occasionally elsewhere: Deuteronomy 4:15, page 435; 5:2, page 296; Numbers 12:2, page 473; 2 Kings 22:19, page 247; 2 Samuel 7:19, page 16; 23:2, page 343; Amos 2:1, page 352. *Allocutus* for *alloquutus* appears in the quotation Joshua 22:8, page 533. *Secutus* for *sequutus*, in 1 Kings 19:21, page 515.

The most interesting and the most informative of these spelling peculiarties is the change from *quum* to *cum*. I have noted a large number of occurrences of *quum* spelling and its variant *cum*; that is, both forms of Tremellius's constant *quum* occur throughout the manuscript. But the occurrence of the *quum* form in the manuscript is virtually restricted to that larger portion of the work written in the bold, masculine hand beginning with the fifteenth chapter of Book One. In the first fourteen chapters of Book One, that portion of the manuscript which has clearly been copied in a different hand from the bolder handwriting in which the remainder survives, I have found only three *quums* unchanged to *cum*. This virtual non-occurrence of the *quum* form in the re-written portion of the manuscript would perhaps indicate that the revisional copying of this portion was done under Milton's direct supervision. At least I wish to suggest that such was the case. Of course, it has always been assumed that the earlier handwriting represents a copy made under Milton's supervision. I am inclined to believe that the partial revision was also done under Milton's direction. The point is interesting in connection with his methods of work after his blindness and consequently complete dependence on amanuenses.

There is one other spelling-variant from Tremellius which must be regarded as a constant for Milton. This is the change of Tremellius's *seculum* to *saeculum*. I have failed to note a single appearance of *seculum* in the manuscript, although there may well be in-

---

[5] The change from *qu-* to *c-* may be observed in *pro populo*, *cf.* p. 47, Ps. 17: 2-3 quotation.

stances of its occurrence. I have made no special search for it, but in my examination of thousands of quotations, scores of which have contained the word, I have not noticed Milton ever using the spelling *seculum*. Apparently, both Milton and his amanuenses spelled the word *saeculum* alike and with considerable care.

This last point brings to mind the most perplexing and the most inevitable of all spelling-variants in any work which is using quotation, the misspellings. Summer, as already stated, has called attention to many of these, but his treatment of them seems to me to have been too dogmatic. Perhaps he was right in using some of them to prove the virtual illiteracy in Latin of the amanuenses; but on the other hand it is doubtful if the most finished Latin scholar could, in copying thousands upon thousands of words in the quotations employed, have copied them all perfectly. Human liability to error is too pronounced and constant a trait, especially in copying work, to allow us to assume because of errors in spelling that the writers were totally unfitted for their tasks. Sumner himself, while a remarkable editor of Milton's document and to whom the student of Milton must forever be indebted, has committed a number of faults in his work, both errors of omission and of commission. These are especially brought to one's attention in comparing the Latin text of the *de doctrina*, prepared first, with his translation in English, prepared from the Latin edition. In the English edition, Sumner was doing exactly what the later amanuenses did for Milton, copying older material and re-checking quotations and citations of Scripture. It is interesting, but not at all suprising, to find that Sumner's English edition of the *Christian Doctrine* is much more reliable for Scriptural citations than is his edition of the Latin *de doctrina*. The reason for this is that the editor could, and evidently did check the later work against the earlier, with greatly improved results for the English translation. I wish to take exception, therefore, to his conclusions regarding the competency in Latin of Milton's amanuenses. He has condemned these unknown persons[6] for having done precisely what he himself, as editor of their work has done: *i.e.* made mistakes in Latin spellings. I wish especially here to point out certain reasons for questioning Sumner's statement regarding Milton's use of a particular edition of Junius-Tremellius. His statement rests upon a sin-

---

[6] Milton's amanuenses are not so much unknown now as they were a few years ago, thanks to Professor Hanford. *cf.* Hanford, J. H., "The Rosenbach Milton Documents," *PMLA*. xxxviii: 290–296.

gle agreement in misspelling between Milton's manuscript and the
1630 Geneva edition of Junius-Tremellius. Now, as previously
stated, there are thousands of misspellings in the manuscript; there
are even a large number of them in Sumner's carefully edited text.
Letters are omitted and inserted erroneously in so many words that
it is useless even to try to list such errors. Because of this, there is
some reason to suspect that Sumner's statement about the edition
Milton used is rather meaningless and unimportant. He said that
Milton presumably used an edition printed at Geneva in 1630, then
mentioned the fact that the spelling of the word on which he based
his contention, is correct in the London edition of 1593. I suspect
that he mentioned this London edition only because, as I have already stated, the early London editions do differ from later editions. I
have used the London edition of 1580, two volumes, quarto; a Hanau edition of 1596; one of Geneva of 1617, folio; of Amsterdam,
1633; and of 1651; besides the suggested Geneva edition of 1630.
The London edition is considerably different in its readings from
those of the Continent; but this is due chiefly to the fact that it is an
early edition, and not to the fact that it is an English edition. The
Genevan edition of 1630 is a more or less standard edition, agreeing
with the other Continental editions just mentioned, except as these
differ among themselves in typographical errors and other minor
details. I see no reason for assuming on the basis of a single miss-
pelled word that Milton confined himself and his amanuenses to any
particular one of these editions. It seems to me that the most one
can say is that he uniformly used an edition later that 1590. There
are too many misspellings in Milton's manuscript to warrant our
picking out one of them, finding that it agrees with a misspelling in a
certain edition of the Junius-Tremellius Bible, and then assuming
that this was the particular edition Milton used. If the matter were
of sufficient importance, a checking of other misspellings with the
spelling in a suspected edition might settle it. I have checked enough
of these misspellings in the manuscript against the Genevan edition
of 1630 to warrant the assertion that the test proposed by Sumner
for this edition will not bear the weight of the assumption.

Returning now to other general characteristics of the Junius-
Tremellius Bible, there is one further peculiarity of Milton's manuscript
citation that should be mentioned here. This is that more often than
not, Milton followed Tremellius's chapter divisions of the Old

Testament. These differ considerably from the standard chapter divisions of the Authorized Version. Sumner, in his edition of the Latin followed rather closely Milton's citations for chapter and verse, disregarding the question of whether or not the citation agreed with Tremellius or was standard. But in the English translation, Sumner has corrected most if not quite all of Milton's citations of Tremellius which do not agree with the divisions of the Authorized Version. In many other ways, Sumner's English translation of the *de doctrina* is much more trustworthy for the Biblical quotations than his Latin edition of the same work.

1. Milton's Announced Changes from Tremellius's Text

Of the genuine and important variants from the Old Testament text of Tremellius to be found in Milton's manuscript, the first to be noted are those which Milton himself pointed out. In a number of places he took exception to Tremellius's translation, the most important being the following. In Chapter ten of the *de doctrina*, Milton, as ruthlessly as a decade or more earlier, was exposing the shams and hypocrisies surrounding marriage and divorce. He attempted the most difficult task of blending Biblical texts to fit his ideas, seeking to support his arguments, especially those in favor of polygamy, by Bible reference. To do this, he deliberately rejected the Tremellius text, saying that it inadequately translated the original. It was then to the original Hebrew he appealed, twice in as many pages citing the reading of Tremellius and rebelling against what seemed to him its purposely distorted and inaccurate translation. The first of these citations is as follows:

Alter locus unde polygamiam esse illicitam disputant, est Levit. xviii. 18. *mulierem ad sororem suam non accipies ad inimicandum et retegendum nuditatem ejus supra eam in vita ipsius.* Hic Junius *mulierem ad sororem suam* vertit *mulierem unam ad alteram,* ut haberet unde polygamiam illicitam esse probaret, interpretatione plane violenta ac rejicienda. (p. 164.)

Except for the phrase *mulierem unam ad alteram,* Milton has not quoted Tremellius here, or any other translator. He pointed out, and rightly, that the Hebrew itself for this passage carries a different meaning from that found in Tremellius's text. Milton has then supplied a closer translation of the Hebrew, thereby of course, and as he intended, lending Scriptural authority to his own argument without, however, in any way distorting the Hebrew. The Hebrew for this passage reads:

ואשה אל אחתה לא תקח לצרר לגלות ערותה עליה בחייה

This might also be translated, *uxorem ad sororem eius non accipies,*
ad lacessendum, ad revelandum nuditatem eius super eam in vitis eius.
Another passage of like nature occurs soon after the one just noted.
Milton here pointed out:

verba ipsa audiamus, quemadmodum reddita sunt ab Junio, [Mal.] cap.
ii. 15. *nonne unum effecit? quamvis reliqui spiritus ipsi essent: quid autem*
unum? Certe ex loco tam obscuro, et quem tot interpretes tam varie vertunt
atque versant, de re tanti momenti velle statuere, et articulum fidei caeteris
imponere, nimis temerarium sane et importunum est. Sed quid tandem
evincit hoc quicquid est, *nonne unum effecit?* unamne foeminam, ut hic
unam duntaxat esse ducendam statueret? at sexus repugnat, immo casus:
caeteri enim omnes fere sic vertunt: *annon unus fecit? et residuum spiritus*
ipsi? et quid ille unus? Ex loco itaque tam obscuro, etc. (p. 166.)

Again, Milton has rejected Tremellius's translation of the Hebrew,
and has provided a translation of his own which he insisted was nearer to the original. The Hebrew for this passage reads:

ולא אחד עשה ושאר רוח לו ומה האחד

This might be more simply translated *et ne unus fecit, et residuum*
spiritus ei, et quid unus? The importance of these passages is that in
both of them, Milton was rejecting Tremellius's text and substituting his own Latin version of the Hebrew original.

2. *Variants Involving Peculiarities of the Tremellius Text*

Sumner's bare assumption that Milton usually employed the
Junius-Tremellius Bible, did not take into account all of the facts
connected with that Bible. For instance, there is a whole group of
Milton's variations from the text of Tremellius formed by the poet's
use of many of the marginal notes occurring in all the folio and in
some of the quarto editions of that Bible. It is quite evident from a
number of the quotations in the *de doctrina* that Milton was using
some of Tremellius's notes. The following examples of the use of
these notes will suffice to indicate the nature of that use, although
this list is by no means exhaustive.

p. 162, Gen. 2:18, Milton, "non est bonum homini esse soli; faciam ipsi
auxilium quasi coram ipso"
Tremellius, "non est bonum esse hominum solum:
faciam ei auxilium commodum ipsi#"
marginal note "#Heb. *quasi coram se ipse sit*"

p. 16, Gen. 6:4,   Milton, "qui erant a saeculo viri"
                     Tremellius, "qui fuerunt jam #olim viri celeberrimi"
                     marginal note, "#Heb. *a seculo viri nominis*"

p. 13, Gen. 6:6,   Milton, "in corde suo"
                     Tremellius, "#animum suum"
                     marginal note, "#Heb. *in corde suo*"

p. 17, Gen. 17:1,   Milton,"*ego sum Deum omnipotens* ad verbum *sufficiens*"
                     Tremellius, "ego sum Deus fortis #omnipotens"
                     marginal note, "#Heb. *Schaddai, id est, sufficiens*"

p. 165, Gen. 26:31, Milton, "juraverunt vir fratri suo"
                     Tremellius, "juraverunt #alter alteri"
                     marginal note, "#Heb. *vir fratri suo*"

p. 135, Lev. 7:18,   Milton, "anima quae comederit ex ea"
                     Tremellius, "#is qui comederit ex ea"
                     marginal note, "#Heb. *anima quae comederit ex ea*"

p. 136, Lev. 7:20,   Milton, "anima quae comederit carnem"
                     Tremellius, "#quisquis autem comederit carnem"
                     marginal note, ":Heb. *anima quae*"

p. 196, Num. 23:14, Milton, "moriatur anima mea mortem justorum"
                     Tremellius, "#moriar ego morte justorum"
                     marginal note, "#Heb. *anima mea moriatur*"

p. 488, Deut. 27:25, Milton, "animam"
                     Tremellius, "#quemquam"
                     marginal note, "#Heb. *animam*"

p. 199, Judges 15:19, Milton, "spiritus"
                     Tremellius, "animae#"
                     marginal note, "#Heb. *spiritus*"

p. 136, 1 Sam. 24:11, Milton, "Animam meam"
                     Tremellius, "#vitam meam"
                     marginal note, "#Heb. *animam meam*"

p. 418, 2 Sam. 7:18, Milton, "sedit coram Jehova"
                     Tremellius, "#restitit coram Jehova"
                     marginal note, "#*consedit*"

p. 168, 2 Sam. 12:8, Milton, "tibi sicut haec et sicut haec"
                     Tremellius, "tibi #haec et talia"
                     marginal note, "#Heb. *sicut haec et sicut haec*"

p. 417, Ps. 32:6,   Milton, "tempore inveniendi"
                     Tremellius, "#tempore obvenerit"
                     marginal note, "#Heb. *tempore obveniendi*"|

p. 196, Ps. 78:50,   Milton, "animam eorum"
                     Tremellius, "#vitam illorum"
                     marginal note, "#Heb. *animam*"

p. 196, Ps. 94:17,   Milton, "anima mea"
                     Tremellius, "#vita mea"
                     marginal note, "#Heb. *anima*"

p. 49, Ps. 95:8,   Milton, "corda vestra"
                     Tremellius, "#animum vestrum"
                     marginal note, "#Heb. *cor*"

p. 489, Ps. 137:8,   Milton, "filia Babylonis"
                     Tremellius, "#gens Babylonica"
                     marginal note, "#Heb. *filia Babyloniae*"

p. 194, Ps. 146:2,   Milton, "dum adhuc ego"
                     Tremellius, "#quam diu futurus sum"
                     marginal note, "#Heb. *quum adhuc ego*"

p. 254, Is. 10:20,   Milton, "in fide"
                     Tremellius, "#fideliter"
                     marginal note, "#Heb. *in fide*"

p. 16, Is. 42:14,   Milton, "silui a saeculo"
                     Tremellius, "silui #jam olim"
                     marginal note, "#Heb. *a seculo*"

p. 135, Zech. 12:1, Milton, "in medio ejus"
                     Tremellius, "#in eo"
                     marginal note, "#Heb. *in medio ejus*"

p. 10, Ps. 14:1,   Milton, "dicit enim stultus in corde suo non est Deus"
                     Tremellius, "dicit stultus cum animo suo# non est
                         Deus"
                     marginal note, "#Heb. *in corde suo*"

p. 19, Prov. 15:11, Milton, "quanto magis corda hominum"
                     Tremellius, "quanto magis animi hominum#"
                     marginal note, "#Heb. *corda filiorum hominis*"

These examples will, perhaps, sufficiently indicate Milton's use of
Tremellius's notes. Such usages as those just noted will also furnish
a basis for supposing that Milton took any note that might occur in
the margins of the Bible he was using. But he used by no means all
such notes. We have already observed his use of the marginal readings of the Authorized Version. Just as with the English marginal
readings, he used some and not others, so with the Latin. At least he
did not consistently follow the practice shown in these selected quo-

tations. Many of his quotations from Tremellius were of passages
which carry a note indicating the Hebrew reading. But very often
Miltoɩ passed this by. Perhaps this was due to his blindness; perhaps it was due to the fact that he was not particularly interested in
all of Tremellius's notes. But the fact remains that he more often
than not neglected to use the notes in his citations. Nor are the
changes in the readings of Tremellius which are due to the notes
uniform throughout the *de doctrina*. There are, as a matter of fact,
many more quotations in the *de doctrina* which show no alteration
whatsoever due to a marginal note, although marginal notes exist
for them, than there are passages quoted which show the influence of
the notes.

The following instances of quotations unaffected by marginal no-
tation in the Tremellius Bible will perhaps suffice. They are but a
handful from hundreds of such unaffected quotations picked at ran-
dom from the *de doctrina*.

p. 145, Ps. 105:25, Milton, "animum eorum"
     Tremellius, "#animum illorum"
     marginal note, "#Heb. *cor*"

p. 461, Ps. 141:3, Milton, "custodiens moderare"
     Tremellius, "#custodiens moderare"
     marginal note, "#Heb. *custodi super haurire labiorum
      meorum*"

p. 485, Ps. 141:4, Milton, "animum . . . cum strenuis"
     Tremellius, "#animum . . . #cum strenuis"
     marginal note, "#Heb. *cor.* & Heb. *viris*"

p. 499, Prov. 11:13, Milton, "animo tegit rem"
     Tremellius, "#animo tegit rem"
     marginal note, "#Heb. *spiritus*"

p. 265, Prov. 12:28, Milton, "ejus immortalis est"
     Tremellius, "#ejus immortalis est"
     marginal note, "#Heb. *nec mors*"

p. 489, Prov. 28:17, Milton, "sanguinem hominis"
     Tremellius, "#sanguinem hominis"
     marginal note, "#Heb. *animae*"

p. 503, Prov. 28:23, Milton, "sequator me"
     Tremellius, "#sequator me"
     marginal note, "#Heb. *post me*"

p. 397, Prov. 28:26, Milton, "animo suo"
       Tremellius, "#animo suo"
       marginal note, "#Heb. *corde*"

ibid: Milton, "sapienter"
       Tremellius, "#sapienter"
       marginal note, "#Heb. *in sapientia*"

p. 514, Prov. 30:17, Milton, "eum juvenes aquilae"
       Tremellius, "eum #juvenes aquilae"
       marginal note, "#Heb. *filii aquilae*"

p. 512, Prov. 31:11, Milton, "animus mariti ejus"
       Tremellius, "#animus mariti ejus"
       marginal note, "#Heb. *cor*"

It is clear from these citations that Milton did not habitually employ Tremellius's marginal notes. This is especially noticeable when it is recalled that the citations listed above represent only a very few of the total number of opportunities for Milton to have made use of marginal notes, but of which he took no advantage whatever. Possibly some of them were overlooked; but so many of the details were apparently worked out with such great care that had Milton really wished to use all the notes, he could as easily have found means to do so as he found means to employ other apparatus. Certainly, he has used enough of them to indicate that he may be supposed to have read them all. But he did not allow every note that occurred to influence his quotation of the passage to which the note was attached. Evidently his selective faculty functioned as much in his use of some notes and his neglect of many more, as like selection did in other aspects of his life and art.

3. Variations from the Tremellius Text for no Apparent Reason

There is next to be discussed a relatively large group of quotations in the *de doctrina* which, for no apparent reason, differ from the text of Tremellius's translation without agreeing with any other. The variation of the quotations constituting this group is never very great, but is nevertheless distinct. Some of these variants consist of changes in phrasings of no particular importance in themselves, such as the following:

p. 531, Ex. 34:12, Milton, "ne sit in etc."
       Tremellius, "ut non in etc."

p. 431, Lev. 19:12, Milton, "ne jurate per nomen meum ad fallaciam
aliquam"
Tremellius, "neque jurate per nomen meum ad fallaciam ullam"

p. 425, Ps. 119:106, Milton, "juravi, et praestabo illud, me servaturum
jura justitiae tuae"
Tremellius, "juravi quod praestabo, me observaturum
jura justitiae tuae"
(This quotation occurs earlier, on p. 191, there
following Tremellius precisely.)

p. 512, Gen. 3:16, Milton, "ipse dominabitur tibi"
Tremellius, "ipse potestatem habeto in te" (1580.)

p. 161, Gen. 3:22, Milton, "ne comedat, et vivat in aeternum"
Tremellius, "ne . . . ut comedat victurus in seculum"

p. 79, Judges 6:22, Milton, "quum vidit Gideon etc."
Tremellius, "quapropter animadvertit etc."

Others of these variants are those quotations in which some of the
words contained in Tremellius's text are dropped out. They may also,
like those just cited, slightly change the phrasing. Examples follow:

p. 88, Gen. 9:16, Milton, "aspiciam, ad recordandum foederis inter
Deum et omnem animantem"
Tremellius, "aspiciam, ad illum, recordaturus foederis
perpetui inter Deum et omnem animantem"

p. 144, Gen. 45:5, Milton, "victus parandi causa me misit"
Tremellius, "victus causa misit me"

p. 316, Ex. 12:15, Milton, "septem dies panes azymos comedite: ipso
die primo amovebitis vetus fermentum e
domibus vestris"
Tremellius, "septem dies panes azymos comeditote,
verum tamen ipso die primo jam amoveritis
vetus fermentum e domibus vestris"

p. 142, Job 9:10, Milton, "facit res impervestigabiles, mirabiles, in-
numerabiles"
Tremellius, "facit res magnas adeoque impervestigabiles et mirabilia adeoque innumera"

p. 407, Job 13:15, Milton, "si enecaret me, in eo sperarem"
Tremellius, "si enecaret non sperarem?"

p. 136, Ps. 7:6,   Milton, "et persequatur animam meam, et capiat"
Tremellius, "persequatur inimicus animam meam et
assequatur"

p. 86, Ps. 68:19,   Milton, "accepisti dona hominibus"
Tremellius, "accipiens dedisti dona hominibus" (but
quoted exactly p. 101.)

p. 401, Ps. 110:3,   Milton, "populus tuus, populus voluntarius"
Tremellius, "populi tui oblationes voluntariae"

One other peculiarity of quotation belonging to this group is the
change, perhaps in a single word, perhaps in more than one word of
a quotation. Sometimes this results in a slight change in sense, but
usually such is not the case. Two or three examples will be enough:

p. 136, Gen. 7:22,   Milton, "omne in cujus naribus halitus spiritus vitae,
ex omnibus quae in sicco, interiit"
Tremellius, "omne cujus in naribus halitus erat spiri-
tionis vitae, ex universis quae degunt in sicco
mortuum est"

p. 465, 2 Kgs. 9:30,   Milton, "fucavit faciem"
Tremellius, "apposito fuco oculis suis"

p. 409, Prov. 3:34,   Milton, "derisores ipse deridet, humilibus autem dat
gratiam"
Tremellius, "derisores ipse deridet, mansuetis autem
dat gratiam"

The variants in this entire group exhibit many of the characteristics
noted in connection with the English quotations. 'Clipping,'
especially, would account for many of these Latin variants. Others
appear to have been slightly adapted in a peculiar manner to the
context, although no apparent purpose is served thereby. All the
quotations belonging here exhibit one common characteristic. All
of them appear to have been slightly paraphrastic. Any one of them
might have been quoted from memory, or at least they seem to be
quotations that have not been fully verified. But one is amazed at
the relatively small number of such quotations. Of course, many quotations not cited here are found throughout the *de doctrina* in which
a single word has been changed from the reading of Tremellius.
But aside from quotations of this nature that are too trivial to notice
in particular, the quotations listed above constitute all, or nearly all

of the sort of variants in which the changes are of the nature indicated under this heading. Their number is exceedingly small.

4. True Paraphrastic Variants from Tremellius

I shall next examine a group of variants which are somewhat like those groups already examined, but which in addition are quite clearly paraphrastic. The more important of these, in fact all of which I can be certain, follow:

p. 297, Deut. 6:25, Milton, "et justitia erit nobis, si observantes fecerimus totem praeceptionem hanc coram Deo nostro quemadmodum praecepit nobis"
Tremellius, "et justitia sit nobis, si observantes fecerimus omnia haec praecepta coram Jehova Deo nostro etc."

p. 21, Judges 13:18, Milton, "quid rogitas de nomine meo, cum sit mirificum"
Tremellius, "ecquid interrogas de nomine meo? fuitque mirificus"

p. 145, 2 Sam. 24:1,   Milton, "incitavit Davidem dicendo, age, numera populum"
Tremellius, "incitasset adversarios Davidem in eos dicendo, age numera Israelem et Iehudam"

p. 156, 1 Chron. 21:16, Milton, "vidit David angelum Jehovae stricto gladio Hierosolymae imminentem"
Tremellius, "David . . . . vidit angelum Jehovae stantem inter terram et coelum, cum gladio suo stricto in manu sua, extenso contra Ieruschalaima"

p. 198, Ps. 49:9,   Milton, "quorum redemptis cessat in saeculum"
Tremellius, "est enim cara redemptio vitae eorum; imo cessat in seculum"

p. 171, Prov. 18:22,   Milton, "qui invenit uxorem, invenit bonum; et consecutus est benevolentiam ab Jehova"
Tremellius, "consequitur bonum qui consequitur uxorem, ut provehit benevolentia a Iehova"

p. 175, Eccles. 9:9,   Milton, "cum uxore quam amas, frui vita juberis omnibus diebus vitae fragilis tuae; quippe quam dedit tibi Deus"
Tremellius, "fruere vita cum uxore quam amas, omnibus diebus vitae vanissimae tuae, quam uxorem dedit tibi Deus"

These quotations are all sufficiently accurate for the sense of Tremellius's text, and they correspond more nearly with his reading than they do with the reading of any other Latin version. They suggest quotations set down from memory, and perhaps, taken together with all the other groups listed previously, they constitute cumulative evidence that Milton drew considerably upon his memory in quoting Scripture. The evidence thus far found of the care he took to make his quotations accurate, his close following for the most part of the text of Tremellius, indicate that in these paraphrastic quotations he trusted his memory because of his virtual certainty of thereby quoting the sense of the passage he had in mind. Such quotation was apparently never the result of his haste, or of his unwillingness to collate with a text. It was rather a drawing on his memory for the substance of a text, the result being a paraphrase of the true text of Tremellius. Several of the quotations cited in this group, however, give but little evidence that he was deliberately paraphrasing or recalling Tremellius. A few of them suggest something else at work. There is no doubt that one or two of the quotations examined in this group were as much paraphrases of the Hebrew original as they were of Tremellius's translation of that original. But in order to show how Milton paraphrased the original Hebrew of the Old Testament, several other groups of quotations in the *de doctrina* must first be examined.

5. Variants from Tremellius Clearly Due to Another Text

Of the minor variants in the *de doctrina*, there remain for discussion those which clearly do not represent deviations or variants from Tremellius's text at all. These apparently were due to some other Latin version of the Old Testament than that of Tremellius.

For Milton's day, or since, when a Latin Bible is mentioned, one thinks at once of the Vulgate. And there is a possibility here that Milton was quoting from the Vulgate, although he never used it regularly. Collation of his quotations proves conclusively that he almost never used the Latin of the Vulgate, and there is no evidence whatever that he ever intentionally quoted from it. For the whole of his Old Testament quotations, in the *de doctrina* or elsewhere in his prose works, there are but two quotations from the Bible that may be even suspected to have been of Vulgate origin. One of these, occurring on page sixty-four of the *de doctrina*, is a quotation from Deuteronomy, the sixth chapter and the fourth verse, *Audi, Israel,*

Dominus Deus noster, Dominus unus est. Now the word *Dominus* in any Latin quotation from the Old Testament may always be suspected to have come from the Vulgate, and always, in order to determine what name of God *Dominus* stands for, one must consult the Hebrew itself. In this case, it reads:

שמע ישראל יהוה אלהינו יהוה אחד

The Hebrew word for which Milton has written *Dominus* is the same יהוה which caused Jerome so much trouble in Exodus, the sixth chapter and the third verse, where he finally transliterated it ADONAI, though usually elsewhere in the Vulgate Old Testament, it is rendered *Dominus*. It was not until the sixteenth century that the word took any other Latin form than these two. But students of Hebrew at the revival of learning took the word יהוה as it stood and considered that the vowels accompanying it belonged to it, although scholars of today agree in holding that the vowels appearing in יהוה are properly the vowels of אדני. That is, אדני ADONAI, is read in the Hebrew whenever the word יהוה occurs in the text. But the Renaissance transliterated the consonants and vowels appearing in the form יהוה and the result was IeHoVaH, which became the Jehovah of the English and other European languages. The first recorded use of the Latin form *Iehova* was in 1516,[7] or considerably before the beginning of Tremellius's translation of the Old Testament in 1560 or 1561. Tremellius, like most translators after 1500, employed the word *Iehova* almost uniformly in his Latin translation wherever יהוה appeared in the Hebrew. The appearance and adoption of the word *Iehova* about the time of the Reformation and consequently of Protestant translations of the Bible, in a way made its use a mark of the Protestant Bible. Tremellius translated the passage already quoted in the following manner: *audi Israel: Iehova Deus noster, Iehova unus est.* The Vulgate reads for the same passage: *audi Israel, Dominus Deus noster, Dominus unus est.* For some reason, Milton quoted this reading rather than that of Tremellius, but it is extremely unlikely that he did so with any conscious intent of following the Vulgate; it is more probable that he quoted from memory of the set phrase *Dominus Deus.* One other instance of the same happening is to be found in the fifth chapter of the *de doctrina,* on page sixty-five in Milton's quotation from the first verse of the one hundred tenth Psalm. His quotation

[7] P. Galatinus, *de Arcanis Cath. Veritatis,* II. lf. x.viii. 1516.

is *dixit Dominus Domino meo*. The same factors are again operating here as in the previous quotation. The Hebrew reads: נאם יהוה לאדני. Milton has used Tremellius's *Domino* in the latter's customary fashion for the Hebrew אדני. But he has changed from Tremellius's translation of יהוה, and used *Dominus*. Tremellius's text reads: *dixit Iehova Domino meo*. The Vulgate reads: *dixit Dominus Domino meo*, which agrees with Milton's quotation. Again, Milton's written quotation agrees with the Vulgate; but again it is improbable that it is so because he was quoting directly from the Vulgate itself, for these are the only two quotatons out of all the several thousands used which agree with the Vulgate rather than with Tremellius's version of the Old Testament. It is safe to say that Milton need never, indeed, can never be suspected of having quoted intentionally from the Vulgate so far as the Old Testament was concerned. Indeed, I have found no other quotations in the whole of the *de doctrina* that can be found to be in agreement with any other Latin version than that of Tremellius, although they may not be in agreement with his. Milton occasionally resorted to other Latin versions than Tremellius for purposes of verifying or disagreeing with that version, but apparently he never quoted from them. It is unfortunate that, so far as is known, no copy of the Junius-Tremellius Bible belonging to him has survived. It would undoubtedly be of more value to the Milton student than his copies of the English Authorized Version that have come down to us. His constant use of it for purposes of quotation indicate a long familiarity with it and almost constant reading.

6. Variants from Tremellius Reflecting the Use of the Hebrew Text

There is another small group of quotations to which I next wish to call attention. This is a group of variants from the text of Tremellius which cannot be explained, as the previous groups have been by anything connected with that Latin version, or with any other. A small number of Milton's variants from Tremellius, without showing the actual use within them of the Hebrew text, do reflect his having consulted that text in connection with them. None of these quotations is of any great consequence, except as it reflects some peculiarity of the Hebrew text. This group differs from any other heretofore discussed, because the quotations within it severally take the forms they do on account of the direct influence of the Hebrew originals. These quotations are not numerous, nor should we expect

them to be, for Milton finally came to depend upon eyes which could
read the Latin of Tremellius better than Hebrew.

I shall first discuss a group of quotations, all of which take the
forms they do because of Milton's deliberate and announced intent
literally to reproduce in Latin the peculiarities of the Hebrew. A
particular grouping by Milton of such quotations is in his discus-
sions of the nature of a Hebrew name of God אלהים (*Elohim.*)
These quotations occur in two passages, the first on page eighteen
reading as follows:

et nomen אלהים etsi plurale sit Hebraice tamen de uno Deo dicitur. Gen.
i. l. אלהים ברא. Psal. vii. 10, et lxxxvi. 10. אלהים חיים et passim: sed et אלה
in singulari dicitur, Psal. xviii. 32. *quis est Deus praeter Jehovam, et quis
rupes praeterquam Dii nostri:* qui versus confirmat singulare et plurale in
hoc nomine idem valere: verum de his plura cap. v.

The other passage occurs on page seventy-eight, and is as follows:

Haec omnia idcirco attendenda, ne quis imperitia linguarum hallucinatus,
voce Elohim cum singulari adjungitur, plurium personarum unam essentiam
significari, continuo sibi persuadeat. Etenim in eo siquid est, quot illa vox
personas, totidem Deos innuit. Quid, quod voci Elohim nunc adjectivum
nunc verbum plurale adjunctum reperitur; quod non personas tantum, sed
etiam naturas significaret plures, si quid hujusmodi in syntaxi positum esset.
Deut. v. 32. *Deorum viventium.* Jos. xxiv. 19. *Dii sancti ille.* Sic. Jer. x. 10.
Gen. xx. 13. *cum me errare facerent Dii.* Quid, quod occurrit etiam nonnun-
quam singularis אלה Deut. xxxii. 18. et saepe alias. Et nomen singulare
אדון Dominus Jehovae adjungitur, Exod. xxiii. 17. Et cum affixo singulari
tribuitur Christo, Psal. cx. 1. *dictum Jehovae* לאדני *Domino meo.* quibus
verbis propheta Christum etiam summi honoris causa Dominum hic
nominatum, et alterum ab Jehova, et, si qua affixo fides, minorem dicit.
At cum Patrem alloquitur, versus 5. mutato affixo אדני inquit, *Dominus
qui sedet ad dextram tuam franget* &c.

The point Milton was making in both of these passages is that the
Hebrew name for God, אלהים (*Elohim*) though plural in form, is
singular in meaning. He noted its appearance in both plural and
singular forms, even supplying one quotation from the Hebrew
which contains the word in both forms, properly recognized by the
Hebrew syntax. Everything Milton has said about the Hebrew use
of the word is perfectly true, and his statements are accurate.

אלה is clearly a singular in Deuteronomy xxxii:18, and לאדני
in Psalms cx:1, is a plural construction with pronomial suffix. He

could have known this, however, only by noting the fact while reading
the Old Testament in the original Hebrew. No Latin version of the
Old Testament even suggests such a treatment as exists in Hebrew of
the word אלהים applied to Deity. Tremellius's Latin reads: *quis est Deus
praeter Iehovam, et quis rupes praeterquam Deus noster*. The Vulgate
and other Latin versions have the same or very nearly the same
reading, as they should, for except in the original Hebrew, there is no
necessity for the distinction between singular and plural such as is
contained therein. There is no need here to suggest the influence of
commentators upon Milton's discussion of this point, for he supplied
references direct to the use of the Hebrew words themselves.

But the chief importance of these quotations is that they exhibit
Milton employing the Hebrew text of the Old Testament directly.
In the use of explanation of single words he has done this in several
other places in the *de doctrina*, particularly in the following instance:

p. 17, Jer. 32:18,   Milton, "Deus est maximus, potentissimus, et El
                      Elion"
                      Tremellius, "Deus est maximus potentissimus, et
                      Jehova exercitum" Hebrew, האל דגדול הגבור
                      יהוה צבאות (El Elion)

Other instances of Milton's direct use of the Hebrew of the Old
Testament will now be discussed, each quotation showing a variation due to the use of the Hebrew original being treated separately.

Such a quotation is the following:

p. 205, Gen. 49:10,   Milton, "donec venerit Filius ejus"
                       Tremellius, "usquedum venturus erit filius ejus"

The variation in this particular quotation from Tremellius is of no
particular consequence. But the same reference is again quoted on
page two hundred thirteen in the following form: *usquedum venturus
est Silo*. It will now be noted that neither quotation follows Tremellius, although only in the second is the change particularly noticeable.
The second quotation, differing much more markedly from Tremellius than the first, shows what was taking place. The Hebrew original
of the verse was in Milton's mind, affecting his quotation, probably
but not certainly in both cases. The Hebrew for the verse reads:

עד כי יבא שילה

Keeping to a Latin translation for purposes of comparison, this may
be translated, *usque quo* (or) *usque dum veniat Silo*. In translating

the Hebrew verb יבא, a *qal* imperfect, as a passive, Milton was probably following Tremellius. But this was a small matter. The important change is in the second quotation. Milton used the Hebrew שליה *Silo* or *Shiloh* here, and this usage, together with the fact that he twice quoted the passage in a different manner from Tremellius's, is sufficient for our purposes here which are to point out, by means of this quotation, that he distinctly had the Hebrew original of the passage in mind in both cases of quotation. The reasons for his use of *Silo* need not detain us, as many of the older commentators will furnish full discussion of the matter. The expression שילה *Silo*, which Tremellius has translated figuratively, Milton translated literally.

The same kind of variation from the Latin of Tremellius is seen again:

p. 15, Ex. 3:14,   Milton, "sum qui sum"
                    Tremellius, "Eheje qui sum"

The Hebrew of this passage reads: אהיה אשר אהיה Tremellius here has transliterated into *eheje* the Hebrew verb. There is no particular point in doing this, for if the verb means *sum* in the second instance, it certainly does in the first. Milton has rejected Tremellius's usage, and used *sum* for both the Hebrew verbs, as well he might.

A variation of minor importance occurs in the following:

p. 512, Ex. 4:25,   Milton, "vir sanguinum es mihi"
                     Tremellius, "sponsus sanguinum es mihi"

The difficulty here is in the Hebrew word חתן, which means *husband* clearly enough. Just why Milton objected to Tremellius's *sponsus* is not clear. The rest of Milton's quotation is in complete agreement with both Tremellius and the Hebrew original. The latter reads כי חתן דמים אתה לי. This may be translated: *quia sponsus sanguinum es mihi.*

An echo from the divorce controversy occurs in the following:

p. 490, Ex. 20:14,   Milton, "non moechaberis"
                      Tremellius, "non scortator"

Milton has clearly attempted to remedy here a gross mistranslation of the seventh commandment. He has corrected Tremillius's translation and shown that the commandment did not forbid coition but adultery. The Hebrew reads: לא תנאף *non adulterabis*. The difference between *moechaberis* (*commit adultery*) and *scortator* (*fornicate*) contained Milton's whole point, and the reading represents his own translation.

Another more exact translation than that furnished him by Tremellius occurs:

p. 163, Ex. 20:17,   Milton, "non concupisces domum"
                       Tremellius, "non concupiscito domum"

The Hebrew for this reads לא תחמד בית and Milton's *concupisces* is precisely the same as the Hebrew תחמד. The point is small, but another instance of a somewhat closer following of the Hebrew occurs

p. 37, Ex. 32:33,   Milton, "eum qui peccat in me, delebo de libro
                       meo"
                       Tremellius, "eum qui peccaverit mihi, delerem de
                       libro meo"

The difference here is small, but the Hebrew reading is אשר חטא לי אמחנו מספרי, almost literally, *qui peccat in me, delebo eum de libro meo*.

Another more faithful adherence to the Hebrew occurs:

p. 135, Lev. 5:2,   Milton, "cum anima tetigerit etc."
                      Tremellius, "quum quispiam tetigerit etc."

The Hebrew for this reads: או נפש אשר תגע, literally, *vel anima quae tetigerit*. Milton has retained the Hebrew word נפש *anima*.

On page four hundred forty-one, Milton discussed the meaning of the Hebrew verb קלל, and deliberately cited meanings for it from various Scriptural passages in which it was used. All of these seem to mean *to condemn utterly* or *to utter impiously*. In this way, he seemed once or twice to be deliberately trying to employ different words for the Hebrew text from those used by Tremellius. One becomes conscious in reading his slightly altered quotations that he was 'glossing' Scripture. Significant here is the fact that he was glossing the Hebrew directly. One such gloss is the following:

p. 441, Lev. 24:14,   Milton, "educite execratorem"
                        Tremellius, "educito blasphemum"

Another much closer rendering of the Hebrew than that found in Tremellius occurs in the following:

p. 245, Num. 11:18,   Milton, "sanctificate vos in crastinum"
                        Tremellius, "parate vos in crastinum"

The Hebrew for this reads: התקדשו למחר, literally, *sanctificate vos in crastinum*, Milton's word being a more literal translation of the Hebrew than that of Tremellius.

That Milton was often thinking of the meaning of the Hebrew and was sometimes not particularly concerned with following Tremellius precisely is perhaps best attested by the following quotation:

p. 413, 1 Sam. 13:13, Milton, "stulte fecisti"
Tremellius, "stulte gessisti"

But the same expression was copied in complete agreement with Tremellius on page five hundred two, and Milton was doubtless concerned mainly with conveying the sense of the Hebrew נסכלת, which means *to play the fool*.

Another more literal translation of the Hebrew than in Tremellius occurs:

p. 416, 1 Kgs. 3:11, Milton, "tibi intelligentiam ad audiendum judicium"
Tremellius, "tibi discretionem ad intelligendum judicium"

The Hebrew for this passage is לך הבין לשמע משפט, literally *tibi intelligentiam ad audiendum judicium*. The change made by Milton is very slight, but in the direction of the Hebrew original.

Another instance of the same nature occurs:

p. 288, 2 Chron. 15:2, Milton, "invenietur a vobis"
Tremellius, "praesto erit vobis"

The Hebrew back of this is ימצא לכם, which is precisely *invenietur a vobis*, although the difference between this and Tremellius is small. Another similar instance is

p. 344, Nehem. 9:3, Milton, "surrexerunt"
Tremellius, "illis erectis"

Milton has preferred to translate literally the Hebrew verb ויקומו.

In the following, there is a clearly marked adherence to the Hebrew; and an illuminating example of Milton's exegesis:

p. 154, Job 4:18, Milton, "angelis suis tribuit stultitiam"
Tremellius, "angelis suis appositurus lucem"

The Hebrew for this reads ובמלאכיו ישים תהלה. Both Milton and Tremellius have translated ובמלאכיו by the phrase *angelis suis*, which is clear enough. But the Hebrew phrase ישים תהלה has caused

trouble here. The difficulty lies in תהלה, which is a perplexing word
in Hebrew. It may be from the root הלל *to shine*, as Tremellius has
taken it to be in which case his translation *appositurus lucem* is quite
right. But the word may also be from another root (תהל), which does
not occur in any other form in Hebrew. Commentators have puzzled
over the word תהלה for centuries, without much success. But the
important consideration here is what Milton has done in this particular quotation, for on page one hundred thirty-four he quoted the
whole expression exactly according to Tremellius, *angelis suis appositurus lucem*. On page one hundred fifty-four, however, he has
not followed Tremellius, but has used another meaning for the Hebrew תהלה. That is, this passage had been noted by Milton as one
offering difficulties. In one case, he followed Tremellius; but in the
other he supplied a different translation. In this second use of the
quotation, he rejected Tremellius's reading and supplied one of his
own which is almost completely opposed in meaning to Tremellius.
He could only have done this after a consideration of the original
תהלה and what it meant in the Hebrew. The fact that many commentaries accessible to him pointed out the meaning of תהלה as
stultitiam would also have had its effect in determining which meaning
he chose. But to admit the influence upon him of such commentaries
is but to emphasize his knowledge of the Hebrew original of the
passage, for the commentaries were based upon discussion of the
nature of the Hebrew root of the word תהלה.[8]

---

[8] A typical comment on this verse, written near the close of the 16th century,
is that of John Mercer, or Mercerus, the French commentator. I quote from the
1573 edition of his commentary on Job. "*Et in angelis ponit stoliditatem* ac vanita-
tem, id est, reperit, ne putes Deum quicquam stolidi in angelis ponere. Durius
vertit noster interpres pravitatem: unde nostri collegerunt haec de Satana &
malignis angelis dici, qui ex gratia & statu perfecto in quo erant, culpa sua deci-
derunt. Sed simplex sensus est de angelis ipsis etiam bonis per se sumptis, qui si
cum Deo conferantur, aut si eos secum Deus conferat, non habens rationem eorum
quae in illis posuit, & dotium ac donorum quae in illos contulit, & quibus eos
exornavit & illustravit, inveniat eos stolidos, var.os & mancos. Alii תהלה *stoliditatem*, lucem exponunt repetita negatione, nec ponit in illis lucem & splendorem, id
est, non invenit eo splendore ornatos quo alioqui ornati sunt, si per sese eos con-
sideret sine gratia quam cum illis communicavit. Sane quicquid habent angeli, a
Deo habent. Ac omne ens quod ab alio suum esse & perfectionem accipit, illo sit
imperfectius oportet, a quo illud habet. הלל & pro insanire & pro splendere infra
hoc libro reperies, sed malo priore sensu. Erit autem a ficta radice הלה ejusdem
significationis cum הלל, quod interdum contrariam habet significationem ei qua
significat laudare, & erit formae תרמה fraus. Est autem argumentum a majori.
Hoc enim mox ad imperfectionem hominum accommodat."

One of the most characteristic and enlightening variants occurring in the *de doctrina* is the following:

p. 192, Job 5:7,   Milton, "homo ad aerumas natus est, ut scintillae
                     rursum evolant"
                     Tremellius, "homo ad molestiam edatur: ut scin-
                     tillae prunarum in altum evolant"

At first glance, this quotation appears to deserve but little more
attention than hundreds of other variants I have listed in collating,
but have not included in this discussion. These others vary from
Tremellius in such slight ways, or are readily comprehensible, that
except for an editor, they can have no interest. But this quotation
from Job is both interesting and informative. It is Milton's rendering or reading for a very well-known Biblical passage. So well known
was it to him that he made no attempt here to follow Tremellius or
any other Latin translation. He knew the meaning of the Hebrew
perfectly well, and consequently supplied his own Latin version for it.
The Hebrew for this verse is כי אדם לעמל יולד ובני רשף יגביהו עוף
or literally *enim homo ad laborem* (עמל means *work* or *trouble*, that
with which man was cursed) *natus est; et filli prunae elevabunt* (or
evolant) *altum.* Milton has gone astray with *rursum;* but his reading
is his own. He has trusted to his understanding of the verse in Hebrew and produced his own Latin translation.

The same thing occurs again in another quotation:

p. 135, Job 32:8,   Milton, "certe spiritus hic in homine, et halitus
                      Omnipotentis facit eos intelligentes"
                      Tremellius, "profecto spiritus ille in mortali: et
                      afflatus omnipotentis efficit eos intelli-
                      gentes"

Almost precisely the same factors have operated here as in the
quotation previously cited. Milton has again drawn on his knowledge
of the Hebrew original of another very familiar passage and produced
his own reading. It is as near to the Hebrew as that of Tremellius,
but, as before, no better. But again, it is his own.

A different kind of variant is the next to be noted:

p. 77, Ps. 8:6,   Milton, "minorem diis"
                    Tremellius, "minorem angelis"

This is one of the passages which Milton cited in order to point out
the plural nature of the name אלהים (*Elohim.*) He has followed the

Hebrew, however, in his translation, rather than Tremellius. The Hebrew original of the passage reads: ותחסרהו מעט מאלהים. This has recently been translated, "and thou didst make him lack little of God."[9] There can be no doubt of the superiority of Milton's translation over that of Tremellius; nor can there be any doubt of his use of the Hebrew original here.

A peculiar variant is found in the following:

p. 132, Ps. 16:11,   Milton, "voluptates aeternae ad dextram tuam"
                       Tremellius, "amoenissimorum: dextra tua in aeter-
                           nitatem"

The change from Tremellius is not great, and the sense is the same as the Hebrew נעמות בימינך נצח, literally, *jocunditates in dextera tua perpetuo*. The peculiarity of the quotation consists in the fact that it appears again on page three hundred eighty-four, exactly following Tremellius. It is another of those passages for which, apparently, Milton felt perfectly capable of supplying his own Latin translation. Another of similar nature is

p. 274, Ps. 19:13,   Milton, "atque a contumaciis cohibe servum tuum,
                           fac ne dominentur in me, tunc integer
                           (sive) perfectus ero, insonsque defectione
                           magna"
                       Tremellius, "tum a contumaciis subtrahe servum
                           tuum, ne dominentur in me; tunc integer et
                           insons ero a defectione magna"

The variation here is negligible; but again the same quotation on page four hundred three follows Tremellius precisely.

The following variant is also characteristic:

p. 63, Ps. 82:6,   Milton, "filii Altissimi vos omnes"
                     Tremellius, "filii excelsi vos omnes"

Milton quite evidently had settled upon *Altissimus*, the *Most High*, as the proper translation of the Hebrew phrase בני עליון כלכם. Attention has been called above to his use of the term *El Elion*, when, on page seventeen, translating the Hebrew, the expression occurring in apposition with *Deus maximus*, in the eighteenth verse of the thirty-second chapter of Jeremiah, *potentissimus* obviously

---

[9] Brown, Driver, and Briggs, *Hebrew and English Lexicon of the Old Testament*, Boston and New York, 1907, p. 341a.

means *altissimus*. Milton used the same expression in English in the metrical translation of the eighty-second Psalm, and again in *Paradise Lost* I:40.

The selection of a different verb, *vastate*, for Tremellius's *nudate* for the Hebrew השדודה is seen on page four hundred eighty, in the quotation from the eighth verse of the one hundred thirty-seventh Psalm.

Closer adherence to the Hebrew is seen in the following:

p. 196, Ps. 146:4, Milton, "in humum suam"
    Tremellius, "in terram suam"

The Hebrew is לאדמתו, the word אדם having special reference to soil. But the whole clause is different:

    Milton, "redit homo in humum suam"
    Tremellius, "revertitur in terram suam"

Another similar variant to these occurs:

p. 8, Dan. 3:16,   Milton, "ut respondeamus tibi de hac re, non sumus solliciti"
    Tremellius, "ut respondeamus tibi, non sumus sollicti de hoc negotio"

The slight disregard for Tremellius here is in marked contrast to the fidelity with which the same reference is quoted on page four hundred seventy-four, and again on page five hundred thirty.

This relatively small but highly significant group of quotations, which vary from the text of Tremellius in the direction of the Hebrew original, yield several facts concerning Milton's attitude toward Scripture, and his use of it.

For one thing, his variation from Tremellius is not constant, even for the same texts in different quotations. Sometimes his reading for a given verse of Scripture differs from Tremellius; but often in another use of the same quotation, Milton will quote Tremellius exactly. There are two different ways of regarding this fact. On the one hand, it is well known that students and translators of the Bible during the Middle Ages and Renaissance who knew the Bible in its original tongues, felt no hesitancy in quoting a verse in Latin in a form which gave the sense only, making no effort to have it agree with any particular Latin version. The same verse might be cited in slightly different ways almost every time it was written or paraphrased in Latin. Milton undoubtedly felt himself to be master of the original texts of Scripture, as he announced in the dedication of the *de doctrina*. His variants from Tremellius which tend toward the Hebrew original might be explained on this basis.

But consider his other variant readings from the text of Tremellius. They appear to vary from Tremellius on no fixed plan; sometimes the variant is one of a word only, and that in Latin. Sometimes there is but a change in word-order. Again, it may be an attempt at securing a closer approximation of the original, either by using Tremellius's notes, or by recourse to the Hebrew text itself. Often the quotation appears almost like a Latin paraphrase of the Hebrew. But no one of these types of variations seems to predominate, nor does any of them appear to have been used systematically. The reasons for this were the various conditions under which Milton worked at the listing of Biblical quotations for the work, and under which they were finally arranged in it. Milton was and had been blind, presumably for some time before the completion of the whole project.[10] But the work of assembling and arranging the quotations must have been started years before its final completion. I dare say the beginning of the task was as early as the plans for an epic found in the Trinity College manuscript. Thus the collecting of Biblical passages must have gone on from before his blindness until some time near the end of the Interregnum.

To account for the variants from standard Biblical versions among these quotations, and, equally important, their sporadic appearances throughout the *de doctrina*, all the facts learned about Milton's use of Biblical quotations must be kept in mind.

We have been able to discover, on the basis of his dated works, that after his blindness he tended much less to deviate either from the text of the Authorized Version for English or from Tremellius for Latin quotations than before.[11] To the casual observer of Milton, it would seem, perhaps, that he, like any other person who became blind, would rely more greatly upon his memory after his blindness than before, and thus his quotations show a greater tendency to

[10] Hanford, J. H., "The Date of Milton's *De doctrina Christiana*," *Studies in Philology*, XVII: 309 ff. This work is a carefully considered resumé of the possibilities of the date. The time arrived at, *ca.* 1657, is acceptable, of course, only as a date at or near completion of the work. Milton's own prefatory statement, together with the nature of the work, would require the actual work of compilation to have occupied many years.

[11] *cf.* Chapter IV.

deviate from a standard text. But for Milton, as we shall see, such was not the case. After his blindness, he was forced to be more careful than before of the accuracy of the quotations now written down by his amanuenses. This was like him—the greater the obstacle, the more fiercely he rose to meet and overcome it. So with his use of Biblical quotations, after his blindness he ceased almost entirely the use of quotations of any nature other than those in faithful agreement with a standard text. Instead of dictating his own version or translation of a Scriptural passage to his amanuenses, he forced those unhappy scribes accurately to copy the text involved from a version that was familiar to them, either the Authorized Version or Tremellius's Latin. Milton used his memory, we may be sure, in checking the correct and accurate reading of these passages as they were read to him by the copyists.

Thus the various quotations in the *de doctrina* of the same Scriptural passage, in one instance agreeing with the Tremellius text entirely, and in another disagreeing, represent Biblical passages set down at different times. The variant quotations in the *de doctrina*, almost without exception, may be assigned, on the basis of the variants in the dated works, to the period of Milton's life before his blindness. In other words, I am inclined to believe that the variations from the text of Tremellius which appear so sporadically in the *de doctrina*, were made before 1651 regardless of when they were inserted in their present positions in the work. This would account for two or more uses of the same Biblical passage showing a change in one and not in the others, which amounts to nothing more than saying that many of the Biblical quotations in the *de doctrina* were compiled before Milton's blindness and many of them after he became blind.

The evidence from the references and quotations of the Old Testament in the *de doctrina* which vary from Tremellius's text, points towards Milton's strong tendency at some period of the compilation to rely upon his knowledge of and familiarity with the Hebrew original. The large bulk of the quotations are taken literally from Tremellius; but there exists a sufficient number of variants to indicate that Milton often departed from Tremellius's reading. Before his blindness, he was certain enough of his Old Testament to be relatively independent of Tremellius. His amanuenses were apparently not so independent. The larger portion of these variants are sufficiently indicative of a tendency toward the Hebrew to warrant the assertion that most, if not all of them, are variants supplied by Milton, not errors in copying, garblings by an amanuensis, or misunderstandings of the text. These latter types of variants have been sufficiently discussed by Sumner to point out how relatively rare and yet discernible they are.

The text of the Old Testament canon has been so standardized since the time of the Massoretes of about the ninth century that it is unnecessary to speculate upon the particular edition of the Hebrew Milton used. I have surmised elsewhere that it was probably the Buxtorf Hebrew Bible printed at Basel in 1620.

7. Milton's Latin Apochrypha

Although it will add little to the present discussion, no account of Milton's use of the Bible would be complete which failed to take account of his quotations from the Apocrypha and the New Testament.

He made but five references to the Apocrypha in the *de doctrina*, and quoted but three of these. These three agree entirely with the Latin translation by Junius from the Greek in which the Apocryphal books are preserved. None of these quotations even suggests any other version than that of Junius. Milton's Latin Apocrypha was, therefore, at least so far as the quotations in the *de doctrina* are concerned, the Latin version to be found in the Junius-Tremellius Bible.

8. Milton's Latin and Greek New Testament

I have collated all of Milton's quotations from the New Testament which appear in the *de doctrina*, and all which appear elsewhere in his works. The great majority of these quotations, but by no means all, agree with what came to be the standard New Testament version for the Junius-Tremellius Latin Bible. As I have already explained, this was Beza's Latin translation of his own Greek text. This was added to Tremellius's translation of the Old Testament, thus making a much more acceptable Bible than had been the case when only Tremellius's translation of the fragmentary Syriac had served for the New Testament.

The great majority of Milton's quotations in the *de doctrina* from the New Testament agree with the Latin version of Beza. In certain editions of the Junius-Tremellius Bible, Beza's text of the Latin New Testament is on a two-column page, Beza's text in one column being paralleled by Tremellius's translation of the Syriac in the other.

There occurs at least one quotation from the New Testament in the *de doctrina* which proves that Milton was using an edition of the Junius-Tremellius Bible which contained these two New Testament Latin texts in parallel columns. On page fifty-nine, Milton quoted the fifth verse of the first chapter of Hebrews as follows:

nam cui dixit unquam angelorum, Filius meus es, ego hodie genui te. Ac rursum, ego ero ille in Patrem, et ille erit mihi in Filium.

The Beza text for the same passage reads:

nam cui dixit unquam angelorum, Filius meus es tu, ego hodie genui te? Ac rursum ego ero ei Pater, et ipse erit mihi filius?

The change here is so slight that it appears to have been of little or no significance. But actually on this quotation rest two facts of some impoitance in connection with Milton's use of the Junius-Tremellius Bible. What actually took place in this quotation is apparent when it is noted that Milton followed Beza quite faithfully until the word *genui* was reached and passed. From that point on, there was a good physical reason for the slight change in the quotation.

It so happened in the folio editions of the Junius-Tremellius Bible that this particular verse appears at the very bottom of a page, so far as the text is concerned. The last word in the text on that particular page in Beza's version is *genui*. In the dual-versioned New Testament of the folio edition, Beza's translation always occupies the outside column of the page. That is, when a reader is confronted by the open Bible, the right-hand page bears Beza's translation in its right-hand column. But when the page is turned, and then becomes the page on the reader's left in the open book, Beza is still on the outside of the page, but is now on the reader's left. This is sometimes confusing, as I myself found in using the folio edition, for one must orientate one's self after turning each page, indeed when passing from one page to another. For the passage cited, the Beza portion begins in the folio edition at the bottom of the right-hand page, continues to the end of it terminating at the word *genui*. The reader then turns the page, and the Beza column is now where the Tremellius column was, and the Tremellius has taken the place of the Beza. For this reason, it is necessary to glance at the Tremellius reading for the verse we have quoted above. It reads as follows:

cui enim ex Angelis unquam dixit Deus, Filius meus es tu ego hodie genui
/ te? Ac rursum, ego ero ille in patrem et ipse erit mihi in filium?

The change from Beza here is very slight, but it is evident that up to
the indicated break, Milton did not use Tremellius. But after the
break, the similarity is much more striking between Milton's quotation and Tremellius's text than between the former and Beza's text.
What happened here was that the amanuensis made the very easy
shift from the Beza text that was being copied before the page was
turned, to the Tremellius text, which occupied the same relative
position after the page was turned, with the result as we see it.
That this is what happened is almost certain, for the same reference
is also quoted on page twenty-nine, where the reading is altogether
that of Beza.

Two facts are, therefore, certain about the form of the Junius-
Tremellius Bible Milton actually used. The first is that he used a
folio edition. This would have meant an edition with notes, and
would establish his use of them in those quotations previously
pointed out. The fact that he used a folio edition establishes the second fact concerning the Bible he used. This is that it was an edition
which printed both Beza's and Tremellius's versions of the New Testament.

Other appearances of Tremellius's version of the New Testament
are apparent in some of Milton's quotations; but no other so clearly
indicates the possibility of confusing Tremellius and Beza as does
this one.

By far the greater number of the New Testament quotations in the
de doctrina agree with Beza's Latin text. I shall now discuss the
variations from Beza's text.

1. Quotations Agreeing with Other Versions than Beza's

The first group of variants from Beza's text is made up of those
quotations which agree with some other Latin Version of the New
Testament than his. Some of the variants agree with Tremellius's
text of the Syriac. It seems unnecessary to list any part of these here,
the one already dealt with being almost the only one that yields any
important information.

There is, however, a much larger number of quotations from the
New Testament than from the Old which agree with the Vulgate. I
have checked a score or more agreements with the Vulgate which can

not be accidental, but which, like those relatively fewer Old Testament agreements with the same version, do not certainly indicate that they are directly from it. They are too few in number to do so, and appear rather to have been quoted from memory, or perhaps were put down at times when the Vulgate was the version most accessible . at the moment. Several of them are undeniably identical, as the following will demonstrate:

p. 17, Titus 1:1, Milton, "qui non mentitur Deus"
Beza, "Deus ille mentiri nescius"
Vulgate, "qui non mentitur Deus"

The same phrase from the same verse appears again on page two hundred fifty-five, and on page two hundred sixty-one the same reference is made in which a different portion of the verse is quoted. Both of these other quotations agree quite clearly with Beza. A similar agreement with the Vulgate occurs:

p. 31, Eph. 1:5, Milton, "praedestinavit nos ad adoptionem"
Beza, "praedestinavit nos quos adoptaret"
Vulgate, "praedestinavit nos in adoptionem"

The difference here is small, but on page thirty-five the same phrase is quoted with *in* in place of *ad*, making the agreement with the Vulgate complete. But again on page two hundred seventy-six, more of the verse is quoted, including the above phrase, and the quotation agrees entirely with Beza. A few others follow:

p. 32, Jude 4, Milton, "olim praescripti ad hoc judicium"
Beza, "olim praescripti ad hanc damnationem"
Vulgate, "olim praescripti in hoc iudicium"

p. 35, 1 Cor. 2:7, Milton, "loquimur sapientiam Dei in mysterio, quae abscondita est, quam praedestinavit Deus ante saecula ad gloria nostram"

Beza, "loquimur sapientiam Dei latentem in mysterio, id est, occultam illam, quam praefinierat Deus ante secula ad gloriam nostram"

Vulgate, "loquimur sapientiam Dei in mysterio, quae abscondita est, quam praedestinavit Deus ante saecula ad gloriam nostram"

Milton has Beza's verb *praefinio*, in other uses of the same reference on pages twenty-two, twenty-three, and one hundred twenty-four. The verb used by the Vulgate, *praedestino*, appears again in the same reference on page thirty-one.

p. 44, Rom. 9:16,   Milton, "non volentis, neque currentis, sed mise-
                         rentis Dei"

                     Beza, "nempe igitur electio non est ejus qui velit,
                         neque eius qui currat, sed ejus qui
                         miseretur, nempe Dei."

                     Vulgate, "non volentis, neque currentis, sed mise-
                         rentis, nempe Dei"

The same verse is also partially quoted on page fifty-two, where the phrase, *sed miserentis Dei* again occurs.

p. 74, Jude 25,   Milton, "soli sapienti Deo servatori nostro gloria
                         esto per Jesum Christum Dominum nos-
                         trum"

                     Beza, "soli sapienti Deo servatori nostro, gloria
                         esto te magnificentia, robur et auctoritas,
                         et nunc et in omnia saecula"

                     Vulgate, "soli Deo servatori nostro, per Iesum
                         Christum Dominum nostrum"

The same quotation again occurs in almost the same form on page two hundred four.

This last quotation is reminiscent of some of the Old Testament variants. For the New Testament as well as for the Old, Milton appears to have been reluctant and unwilling to rest content with Latin translations, however good. In the main, he relied upon Beza for quotations. But, as with the Old Testament, he could and did pass from Beza's Latin to the original Greek whenever occasion demanded. At the opening of the sixth chapter of the *de doctrina*, he quoted the Greek original and supplied his own Latin paraphrase or translation. Citations of the original Greek for New Testament passages are slightly more frequent than citations of the original Hebrew are for the Old Testament. This citation of the Greek original we should naturally expect from Milton. He quite evidently held the Greek of the New Testament to be the ultimate authoritative source form of the New Testament, as he held the Hebrew to be the authoritative text of the Old. Just as for the Old, he ordinarily trusted to Tremellius for quotation, so for the New Testament he ordinarily trusted Beza. But always when he wished he went directly to the Greek original for verification, and citation or quotation.

It is unnecessary to speculate upon the Greek version he customarily employed, for he mentioned Beza's edition of the Greek Testament too many times in the *de doctrina* to admit of any doubt.[12]

9. Other Biblical Texts Milton Employed

Milton referred relatively often throughout his w ..ks to the Aramaic paraphrases of the Old Testament which pass under the name of *Targumim*. In the *de doctrina*, he expressly referred to the substantiation of a text-reading by the *Targum*.[13]

For the New Testament, he has discussed enough variants in the Syriac to indicate very clearly that he employed this version to a considerable extent. In the *Tetrachordon* he referred to the Syriac reading for the thirty-fourth verse of the nineteenth chapter of Matthew, and again in the *Areopagitica* he noted the Syriac for the nineteenth verse of the nineteenth chapter of Acts. In addition to these, there are a number of references to the Syriac in the *de doctrina*. One of these deserves attention.

Milton, on page eighty-two, quoted the twenty-eighth verse of the twentieth chapter of Acts, *ecclesiam Dei, quam per proprium sanguinem acquisivit*. He then added a statement of his own, "verum Syriaca versio non *Dei*, sed *Christi* ecclesiam scribit; ut nostra recens *Domini* ecclesiam." The reference to *recens nostra* puzzled Sumner greatly, and in his English translation, to which, rather than to the Latin edition of the *de doctrina*, he appended his notes and other critical apparatus, he indicated in a footnote that he took this to be a recent English translation. He referred to the editions of the sixteenth century as possible sources of the expression *Domini ecclesiam*. But surely, these would not have been referred to by Milton as *recens*.[14]

---

[12] pp. 68, 82, 90, 122, 168, 201, 350.

[13] p. 213.

[14] *Prose Works of John Milton*, Bohn Edition, vol. IV. p. 112, note 8. Sumner, in the following note, confessed that he was unable to discover the Bible to which Milton referred, "In the list of various readings given in Bp. Wilson's Bible, it is stated that the reading *of the Lord* exists in one of the English Bibles printed by Whitchurch, which was probably the 'recent translation' alluded to by Milton. This printer published many editions of the Bible, separately or in conjunction with Grafton, about the middle of the sixteenth century. The library of St. Paul's

Sumner's work as editor, translator, and annotator was of such a profound nature, as his note indicates, that one hesitates to charge him with error or misunderstanding, but in this particular instance, it seems clear that his fundamental assumption was false. As his note states, he inferred that Milton was referring to a recent English edition of the Bible. This, however, was unwarranted on two counts. Milton was referring in the first part of his statement to a standard edition and translation of the Syriac, and the mere fact that he was writing in Latin would lead one to infer that he was referring to a Latin translation and not an English. Moreover, the Syriac Testament is fragmentary, and therefore has been seldom if ever published in English translation. The standard form in which it usually appeared was as a Latin translation of those portions of the New Testament found in the Syriac, supplemented, as in the Junius-Tremellius Bible, by excerpts from Beza or other Latin translations of those parts missing in the Syriac. Milton was therefore presumably referring to the standard Latin translation of the Syriac, for him the translation of Tremellius done in 1569 at Paris, in the first part of his statement regarding the Syriac, and to some other more recent Latin translation of the Syriac in the second part. This is significant. For, while Biblical versions were frequent in the sixteenth and seventeenth centuries, translations of the Syriac New Testament have been rare. In Milton's day, such a translation would have been of great interest to him.

Instead, therefore, of having hunted for an English Biblical version in which the reading for this verse was *Lord*, Sumner should have hunted for a translation of the Syriac, contemporary with Milton, probably done in Latin, in which the word ܡܫܝܚܐ (Meshiha) had been translated *Domini* or *Domino* and not *Christi*. Such a search is much simpler than Sumner's, for at the time Milton was writing,[15] there had indeed appeared a very "recent" translation

---

contains ten editions published in different years between 1530 and 1560, but the reading alluded to appears in none of them. The libraries of the British Museum, Lambeth, and Canterbury (which latter collection contains about fifty ancient English Bibles and Testaments presented by the late Dr. Coombe) the Bodleian library at Oxford, the University library, and the libraries of Trinity and St. John's Colleges, Cambridge, have also been searched without success for a copy of the edition in question."

[15] Hanford, *op. cit.*, The work was written between 1655 and 1660, probably about 1657.

of the Syriac, which was, of course, the Latin translation printed in
Walton's *Biblia Polyglotta* of 1654 and onward. In this translation,
the phrase ܐܡܝܫܡܕ ܐܬܕܥ (Church of the Meshiha) is rendered
ecclesiam illam Domino, which Milton has adopted by the simple
expedient of changing the dative of reference or possession, *Domino*,
to the genitive *Domini*. So nearly does the date of Walton's work
agree with the most carefully considered dating of the final composition of the *de doctrina*, that Milton's pointing out of the use therein of the word *Dominus* in place of *Christus* is very striking indication
of what he meant by *recens*. The "recent translation," therefore,
would appear, on the dual basis of proximity in time and agreement
of citation, to have been the translation of the Syriac in Walton's
Polyglot; which quite clearly demonstrates that Milton employed
this Bible.

To connect Milton with this Bible is to connect him with Scripture in its various basic texts. But it does more than this. Of the
texts contained therein, for the Old Testament, he himself could
read the Hebrew, the Septuagint, and the *Targumim* directly. For
the New Testament, he could himself read the Greek and the Syriac.
That is, with his own eyesight, he could at all times have read at
least the more important texts of Scripture. But blind, he was restricted to what his readers could read. Before the appearance of
Walton's work, this must have been a serious handicap for him. But
after the appearance of that work, he could secure the reading of any
of the various versions included therein through the Latin translation or paraphrase which accompanied each. Walton's Bible would
therefore have kept open to him after his blindness all the texts of
Scripture he ever could have read before blindness, and in addition,
would have supplied him access through any of his readers who could
read Latin, to the various other versions of Scripture that Walton
printed.

The remainder of Milton's comment upon the reading of the same
passage in Acts, the twenty-eighth verse of the twentieth chapter,
is furthermore most informative concerning all that was involved in
his use of Scripture and more especially in his use of quotations. He
continued as follows:

Neque vero Graecorum codicum certa hic fides est; quorum quinque teste
Beza legunt τοῦ κυρίου καὶ θεοῦ; et suspicatur is τοῦ κυρίου ex margine
irrepsisse; cum proclivius sit suspicari irrepsisse, quod additum est,

καὶ θεοῦ. Neque ex illo Rom. ix. 5. *qui est supra omnes Deus benedictus in saecula, Amen.* Primum enim apud Hilarium et Cyprianum hoc loco *Deus* non legitur; uti nec apud alios patres nonnullos, si qua Erasmo fides: qui etiam ex varia interpunctione, in dubium vocari hujus loci sententiam posse ostendit, utrum de Filio, an potius de Patre intelligenda haec clausula sit.

This passage, together with the citation and comment of the sixteenth verse of the third chapter of the first Epistle of John occurring on page eighty-four as part of the same discussion, makes evident the fact that Milton had at his service and made use of Biblical critical apparatus of some magnitude. Versions, variant readings, commentaries, comparisons of various manuscripts, all the apparatus of the Biblical scholar were known to him. If in his discussion of such passages he settled no textual problems, he at least gave every indication by their citation of having been aware of the best critical practices of his day.

A brief recapitulation of this chapter is sufficient to point out the eminent fitness of Milton to use almost any form of Biblical commentary or other critical apparatus of his time. Certainly, so far as his knowledge of Scripture was concerned, on the basis of his own citation and use of it, all critical appurtenances of the Bible which in any way depended upon a thorough knowledge of the text would have been used by him provided they were available. If knowledge of the Hebrew text of the Old Testament is a requirement for the use of critical apparatus connected with that text, Milton was amply qualified in that respect.

For quotation of the Old Testament, he ordinarily used Tremellius's Latin version, but could and did go directly to the Hebrew itself whenever dissatisfied for any reason with the Latin. He used Beza's Latin translation for ordinary quotation from the New Testament, but continually employed the same editor's Greek text. He quoted from Junius's Latin translation of the Apocrypha, to which he had access in the Junius-Tremellius Bible. The edition of this Bible which he used was the folio, with full notes, and with Beza's Latin translation of the whole Greek New Testament and also Tremellius's Latin translation of the fragmentary Syriac for the same Testament. For English quotations, Milton ordinarily employed the Authorized Version. Whenever he wished, however, he disregarded this and went direct to the originals. He knew and occasionally used the Aramaic Targumim of the Old Testament. He was familiar with intricate problems of exegesis and of the textual criticism practiced in his day. On occasion, he could and sometimes did cite variant readings from various versions and manuscripts. In brief, virtually all of the scholarly apparatus of the Biblical student of his day was actually used by him in his citation and quotation of Scripture. Such a man was admirably equipped to employ rabbinical glosses to the text of the Old Testament.

Milton's Biblical quotations and citations, including those in the *de doctrina Christiana*, have now been examined. The examination has proceeded with special reference to his degree of competency in the knowledge and use of the Old Testament in its original Hebrew. He has been found to have possessed a very thorough and accurate knowledge of the Hebrew text. The best criterion of his competency is the appearance of his own translations and other deviations from standard translations of the original Hebrew, due to a desire on his part for a closer reproduction of the spirit or sense of the original. In addition to this excellent knowledge of the Hebrew original, he has also been found to have possessed an acquaintance with much critical apparatus connected with the Hebrew text. He has also cited the Targums and other Semitic versions of the Old Testament.

The results of this investigation show very clearly that Milton held to the authenticity of but a single text of the Bible. Only the Hebrew original of the Old Testament was the Old Testament so far as he was concerned, and the New Testament was the Greek. No version or translation of the Bible sufficed, although he showed definite preference for a particular English version, the Authorized, and for a particular Latin version, that of Junius-Tremellius. This investigation will show clearly, therefore, that the Bible for Milton was the Bible in its originals, and furthermore it will show with equal clarity his complete familiarity with and mastery of those original texts.

CHAPTER IV

MILTON'S USE OF THE BIBLE BEFORE AND AFTER HIS BLINDNESS, WITH CHRONOLOGICAL INDEX

In the accompanying table or chart, I have arranged a complete list of the biblical citations in Milton's English prose works and in the Latin *pro populo*. These citations are arranged in a chronological order, beginning with the tract *Of Reformation* of June (?), 1641, and terminating with *Of True Religion* of 1673. The first column of the table contains the name of the work in which the citation occurs; the second column indicates that the citation is or is not a quotation. The next column indicates those quotations which agree with a definite biblical text, the Authorized Version for the English quotations, and Junius-Tremellius or occasionally the Vulgate for the Latin. The next column records those quotations which differ from the reading of the Authorized Version if in English, or from Junius-Tremellius if in Latin. The last column records those quotations which have been fitted to Milton's context.

The whole table gives opportunity for quick summary of all the quotations in all Milton's prose works except the posthumous *de doctrina*.

The chief result of this tabulation is to give us definite information concerning Milton's use of Biblical quotations throughout his lifetime. Especially important is the information afforded by the examination of his habit with quotations before and after his blindness. It was to show this difference in Milton's use of Biblical passages before and after his blindness that I purposely arranged the quotations in the chronological order of the works in which they occur.

In order to determine whether Milton changed his manner of using biblical quotations after his blindness came upon him, it is only necessary to consult the tabulation of the quotations.

We know very little about the date of composition of the *de doctrina*, and nothing whatever about the time of collection of the Biblical quotations contained therein, whether before or after blindness. The quotations in the *de doctrina*, therefore, afford no information concerning his procedure with quotations before and after his blindness. For that reason, they are excluded from this tabulation.

But Milton's other prose works are dated, and we know almost precisely when he wrote most of them. Likewise, we know approximately when he became blind, and this date becomes practically certain so far as the writing of his prose works is concerned. Thus, the Latin *pro populo* was undoubtedly the last prose work which he composed with sound eyesight. It was certainly the last prose work written "with his own eyes" in which Biblical quotations appear in any quantity.

It forms, therefore, a sure division between those works which he himself wrote out, and those which he caused to be written out by amanuenses. It marks the important termination of his own free use of Scripture, or of texts which he himself read and wrote out with his own eyes.

Now for a man as well versed in Scripture as Milton was, we might suspect that because of his thorough knowledge of the Biblical text, he would, after his blindness, have depended largely on his memory when quoting Scripture. The tabulation of his use of Biblical quotations throughout his lifetime, because of its chronological arrangement, affords a ready and authentic answer to the question of whether he did draw heavily on his memory in his use of Scripture after his blindness. If the early works be checked for the appearance in them of quotations differing from a standard text, and compared with a like checking of the later works or those written after his blindness, a definite answer can be given to the above question. Let us examine his use of Biblical quotations on this basis.

Those works written by 1651, including the Latin *pro populo*, contain approximately three hundred and fifty Biblical citations, of which about two hundred fifty appear with quotation. Of these, as should be expected, a majority, or over one hundred thirty, which is only a bare majority, agree completely or nearly so with the reading of the Authorized Version or with Junius-Tremellius. Actually in the appended table, there are three hundred forty-six citations with two hundred fifty-four quotations. Of these quotations, one hundred thirty-six agree with one or the other of the standard texts from which Milton usually quoted. This is fifty-three and five-tenths per cent of the whole number of quotations, or only slightly over half.

For the same group of quotations, those cited before blindness, one hundred three are changed in some manner from the standard texts, or forty-six per cent. That is, in the prose works written before blindness, including the Latin *pro populo*, nearly half of the Biblical

quotations are in some manner changed from the reading of the standard texts Milton customarily used and agree with no other version.

Of those changed, thirty-one or twelve and two-tenths per cent,
are fitted to the context of the Miltonic sentences in which they occur.

It would therefore appear that before his blindness Milton felt
extremely free to alter or adapt Scriptural passages to suit himself.
But an examination of the works written before 1652 discloses the
fact that his alteration of Scriptural texts before his blindness was
constant. That is, in the work done shortly before his blindness, and
in that done much earlier, so long as he had his eyesight, there is
about the same amount and degree of alteration of Scriptural texts.
Before his blindness, there is no progressive increase or decrease in
this alteration, the differences in its appearance depending wholly
on what took place in individual works.

After 1651, or after Milton came to depend upon amanuenses for
the work of preparing his manuscripts, there is an immediate change
in his use of quotations. As already stated, there is no tendency toward this change before blindness; it happens very suddenly. After
this date, there appeared in his works one hundred seventy-four citations of Scripture, fifty-one of which are not quoted. My tabulation
shows that one hundred twenty-four actual quotations occur in the
works published after 1651. Of these, one hundred three, or eighty-
three per cent, agree with the text of the Authorized Version, there
being no published works in Latin after that date using Biblical quotations. The remaining twenty-one citations or sixteen and nine-
tenths per cent, differ from the standard reading. Of these which
differ, I find but four which are definitely fitted to a Miltonic context, or three and two-tenths per cent.

These figures are perhaps a little difficult to keep in mind, and
are much more forceful if arranged schematically. For purposes of
comparison and quick reference, I therefore summarize the above
statements in the following short table;

		%
Biblical Citations in Works before Blindness	367	
Cited but not Quoted	92	
Total Quotations before Blindness	285	
Quotations Agreeing with Standard Text	136	47.7
Quotations differing from Standard Text	118	41.4
Quotations fitted to Miltonic Context	31	10.8
Citations in Works after Blindness	179	
Cited but not Quoted	51	

Total Quotations after Blindness	128	
Quotations Agreeing with Standard Text	103	80.4
Quotations differing from Standard Text	21	16.4
Quotations Fitted to Context	4	3.1

	Before Blindness		After Blindness	
Quotations Agreeing with Text	136	47.7%	103	80.4%
Differing from Standard Text	118	41.4%	17	16.4%
Fitted to Context	31	10.8%	4	3.1%

It is clear from these tabulations that after his blindness, there is a marked falling off in the number of changes which Milton made in the Scriptural passages he quoted. The decrease in the total number of changed quotations is about thirty per cent. But the relative percentages of changed quotations before and after blindness are about in the ratio of three to one. That is, after his blindness, Milton changed only about one-third as often those quotations he used as he did before he was blind. He fitted quotations to his context only about one-fourth as often after he was blind as he did before. These two points should indicate very clearly that after his blindness he depended very little upon his memory in quoting from Scripture, being most reluctant to use anything other than the actual reading of an authentic version, the Authorized, except for special cases. He exhibits much more meticulous care for exact quotation of this authentic text after his blindness than he had ever exhibited before he became blind. When, after his blindness, he uses a quotation that does not agree with a standard text, he very infrequently if at all exhibits a willingness to change it slightly. Those quotations examined earlier which were said to be "clipped," those which used marginal variants, and those which were so slightly changed as not to change the sense—all these are missing after his blindness.

There is but one real class of variants discernible after his blindness, and this is represented by the quotation that presents a reading for or a translation of the original Hebrew or Greek which is Milton's own production. The only kind of change that he made from the reading of the standard text, after his blindness, is, therefore, the change that represents his own preferred translation of the original. The significance of this is apparent. Milton insisted on his amanuenses accurately copying the reading of the Authorized Text, except for such passages as he felt to be corrupt or inadequate translations of the originals. In such cases, he supplied his own reading, as he had done throughout his life.

CHRONOLOGICALLY ARRANGED TABLE OF THE BIBLICAL CITATIONS IN THOSE PROSE WORKS PUBLISHED DURING MILTON'S LIFETIME, WITH INDICATIONS OF HOW HE QUOTED THEM.

		Cited but not Quoted	Agreeing with a Standard English or Latin Biblical Translation (Authorized Version or Junius-Tremellius)	Differing from Any Biblical Translation	Fitted to Context
Of Reformation					
John	13:6–10				X
Zech.	14:20			X	
Col.	2:8, 18				X
Prelatical Episc.					
Prov.	24:21			X	
Matt.	5:18			X	X
	7:22, 23			X	X
Gal.	1:8			X	X
1 Tim.	1:3				X
	3:4, 12	X			
2 Tim.	4:3				X
Rem.'s Defense					
Is.	9:15		X		
Jer.	7:15		X		
Ezek.	13:11, 15		X		
John	4:22		X		
	6:27		X		
1 Cor.	10:21	X			
2 Cor.	8:23	X			
1 Tim.	1:3		X		
	3:3				X
	6:8, 9, 10		X		
	:11		X		

2 Tim.	1:6			✗	
	3:16–17		✗		
Titus	1:5			✗	
2 John	11				✗
Rev.	2:10		✗		
Reason of Ch. Govt.					
2 Chron.	15:3, 5, 6, 7		✗		
Prov.	1:20–21		✗		
Is.	52:7		✗		
	66:21		✗		
	:23		✗		
Jer.	15:10			✗	
	20:9		✗		
	:10			✗	
Ezek.	40:	✗			
Zech.	8:10				✗
John	13:16–17		✗		
2 Cor.	10:4–5		✗	✗	
1 Tim.	1:5		✗		
	:18		✗		
	2:1		✗		
	3:14–15		✗		
	5:21		✗		
	6:13		✗		
1 Peter	5:1–6				✗
Rev.	5:5		✗		
	11:1			✗	
Apology					
Is.	56:10–11			✗	
Luke	3:7		✗		
	11:23		✗		
Doct. and Discip.					
Gen.	2:18			✗	
	18:23, 25			✗	
Exod.	21:18, 19, 20, 26	✗			
	34:16	✗			
Num.	5:	✗			
Deut.	7:2, 3		✗		
	7:3, 6	✗			
	13:6, 9	✗			
	19:5	✗			
	22:9, 10			✗	

	24:1		X		
	24:1	X			
	24:4		X		
	25:19			X	
Judges	19:2	X			
2 Chron.	19:2		X		
Ezra	9:2	X			
	10:10, 11	X			
Nehem.	13:30	X			
Ps.	94:20	X			
	119:138, 140		X		
Prov.	2:17		X		
	12:4			X	
	18:13		X		
	21:9		X		
	:19		X		
	27:15		X		
	:16		X		
	30:19, 20			X	
	:21, 23			X	
	:21, 23				X
Eccles.	7:16		X		
	9:9		X		
Cant.	8:6, 7			X	
Is.	10:1		X		
Ezek.	17:19	X			
Mal.	2:16			X	
	2:16	X			
Ecclus.	13:16		X		
	37:27	X			
Matt.	13:52			X	
	19:4, 5			X	
	:4, 5		X		
	:8		X		
	:9		X		
	:11, 12		X		
	:12			X	
Mark	5:31	X			
	10:5	X			
	:7, 8			X	
Luke	16:	X			
Acts	15:10		X		

12

Rom.	2:25		X	
	5:20		X	
	7:10			X
	:12			X
	13:	X		
	:4			X
1 Cor.	7:6		X	
	:9		X	
	:10, 11	X		
	:12		X	X
	:15			X
	:15		X	
	:16		X	
	:24		X	
	:25		X	
	9:8		X	
	13:7		X	
2 Cor.	6:14	X		X
	:14, 15		X	
	:17		X	
Gal.	5:3		X	
Ephes.	4:14, 15	X		
1 Tim.	1:5		X	X
	:8		X	
	2:12		X	
Judgment of M. Bucer				
Mal.	2:15, 16			X
Rom.	7:1, 2		X	
Tetrachordon				
Gen.	1:27		X	
	:28		X	
	2:18		X	
	:23		X	
	:24	X	X	
	9:	X		
Exod.	5:	X		
	21:	X		
	22:17	X		
	34:16	X		
Lev.	18:	X		
	:3			X
Num.	15:39	X		
	30:	X		

Deut.	4:1, 2, 5–8		X		
	:5–8		X		
	7:3, 6	X			
	14:1, 2		X		
	21:	X			
	22:	X			
	24:	X			
	:1, 2		X		
	26:18, 19		X		
	32:4		X		
Judges	19:2	X			
1 Sam.	20:	X			
	19				
2 Chron.	19:2		X		
Nehem.	13:24, 26	X			
Job	9:3	X			
Ps.	34:	X			
	73:26, 27	X			
	94:20	X			
Prov.	2:17	X			
	8:30			X	
	30:21, 23				X
Is.	10:	X			
Jer.	3:1		X		
	31:	X			
Ezek.	17:	X			
Mal.	2:11, 14		X		
	:14	X			
	:16			X	
Ecclus.	25:26	X			
Matt.	5:31, 32		X		
	19:	X			
	:3, 4		X		
	:4, 5, 6		X		
	:7, 8		X		
	:10		X		
Mark	10:3, 5	X			
	:26			X	
	16:	X			
Luke	6:35		X		
	13:15		X		
	:16			X	
	14:	X			

Book	Ref	1	2	3	4
	16:17, 18	X			
	22:36			X	
1 Cor.	5:	X			
	6:7			X	
	7:	X			
	:1		X		
	:10, 11		X		
	:26	X			
	11:3, 7				X
2 Cor.	6:17, 18				X
Gal.	5:1			X	
Eph.	5:24		X		
	:30			X	
	:32			X	
Col.	2:14	X			
	3:18		X		
1 Tim.	1:	X			
	:5	X			
	:5		X		
	5:8		X		
		21			
Ex.	21:8	X			

Colasterion

Book	Ref	1	2	3	4
Deut.	21:14	X			
	24:1	X			
Prov.	21:9, 19	X			
Jer.	13:23			X	

Tenure of Kings

Book	Ref	1	2	3	4
Deut.	17:	X			
	:14			X	
1 Sam.	8:	X			
2 Sam.	5:3			X	
1 Kings	12:16			X	
	:24			X	
2 Kings	11:17				X
1 Chron.	11:	X			
Ps.	51:4		X		
	94:20		X		
Prov.	12:10				X
Is.	26:13	X			
Jer.	48:10			X	
Matt.	20:25			X	
Mark	10:42, 43			X	

Book	Ref	1	2	3	4
Luke	4:6		X		
	13:32		X		
Rom.	13:1		X		
1 Peter	2:13	X			
Rev.	13:	X			

Articles of Peace

Book	Ref	1	2	3	4
Prov.	19:10		X		
	:10		X		
	30:21				X
Eccles.	10:6, 7				X
Zech.	13:3			X	
	:4			X	
	:4		X		
Rom.	11:	X			
2 Cor.	10:4–6			X	X
Jude	3	X			

Eikonoklastes

Book	Ref	1	2	3	4
Gen.	4:13, 14			X	
	9:6	X			
	10:10	X			
	27:34		X		
Exod.	9:27			X	
	10:16			X	
Num.	23:10		X		
	35:31, 34		X		
Judges	17:13		X		
	18:24		X		
1 Sam.	15:24		X		
	:30		X		
	23:7	X			
1 Kings	21:27			X	
2 Kings	6:30, 31			X	
2 Chron.	28:2	X			
Ps.	78:34	X			
	:36, 37	X			
	105:15	X			
	107:40	X			
	149:8			X	
Prov.	28:15, 16, 17		X		
Hosea	7:14, 16		X		
1 Esdras	3:	X			
	4:	X			

Book	Verse				
Matt.	27:4		X		
Acts	8:24		X		
Heb.	12:17		X		
James	4:3		X		
Rev.	17:16				X
Pro populo					
Exod.	18:15		X		
	:19			X	
	:19–20			X	
Num.	12:7			X	
Deut.	4:5		X		
	17:14		X		
Josh.	1:17			X	
Judges	8:23			X	
	15:11		X		
1 Sam.	8:7, 8			X	
	:17		X	X	
	:18			X	
	12:12		X		
	:17			X	
	20:8		X		
2 Sam.	12:5			X	
	:7		X		
	:12			X	
	:13		X		
1 Kings	12:16			X	
	:24		X		
1 Chron.	29:11, 12		X		
	:23		X	X	
Ps.	17:2			X	
	:2, 3			X	
	51:6		X	X	
	94:20		X		
	105:15		X		
	149:8			X	
Eccles.	8:1, 2		X		
	9:19			X	
Is.	45:1	X			
	54:16		X		
Jer.	27:7	X			
	38:5			X	
Hosea	8:4		X		
	13:10, 11			X	

Matt.	6:24	X		
	17:25, 27			X
	20:25–27			X
	22:20, 21			X
Luke	1:51, 52			X
	4:6			X
Rom.	13:1		X	
	:2		X	
	:3			X
	:5		X	
	:7		X	
1 Cor.	7:21, 23		X	
1 Tim.	2:2			X
1 Peter	2:13–15			X
	:16		X	
Rev.	13:2			X
	17:2	X		
	18:9	X		
	19:21	X		

Civil Power

Deut.	17:8	X		
2 Chron.	34:33		X	
Ps.	110:3		X	
Prov.	21:27		X	
Is.	55:1		X	
Jer.	29:24, 26	X		
Matt.	13:26–31		X	
	16:17		X	
	18:16		X	
	:17			X
	23:23	X		
Mark	9:39			X
	16:16	X		
Luke	7:30			X
	12:14	X		
	14:16		X	
	15:4	X		
John	4:21, 23		X	
	6:44	X		
	7:37		X	
	18:36		X	

Book	Reference			
Acts	4:19		X	
	10:15	X		
	15:5			X
	17:11		X	
	26:5			X
	:18		X	
Rom.	12:1		X	
	13:1		X	
	14:4			X
	:5, 23		X	
	:6 (5)		X	
	:9, 10		X	
1 Cor.	1:27		X	
	2:15			X
	:16	X		
	5:5	X		
	:12	X		
	6:1	X		
	:4	X		
	7:23			X
	9:19		X	
	11:18, 19			X
	16:22		X	
2 Cor.	1:24		X	
	3:17		X	
	9:7		X	
	10:	X		
	:3–6		X	
Gal.	4:3–10		X	
	:3, 9, 10	X		
	:10		X	
	:26, 31		X	
	:31		X	
	5:1		X	
	:13		X	
	:20			X
	:22, 23	X		
	6:2		X	
	:4, 5		X	
Col.	2:8, 16	X		
	:8, 10, 14, 16		X	
	:16	X		

Book	Ref				
2 Thess.	2:4			X	
1 Tim.	1:20				
Titus	3:10			X	
James	4:12		X		
1 Peter	5:2, 3		X		
1 John	3:20	X			
Rev.	2:20		X		
	3:18		X		
	22:17		X		

Remove Hirelings

Book	Ref				
Gen.	14:	X			
	28:22	X			
	38:8	X			
Lev.	27:30		X		
Num.	18:21, 24, 28				X
	:30, 31, 32				X
	:28, 29, 32	X			
Deut.	14:23		X		
	14:24–26	X			
	:28, 29	X			
	26:12, 13	X			
1 Sam.	2:12		X		
Is.	49:23		X		X
	56:11		X		
Matt.	9:35	X			
	:38		X		
	10:7	X			
	:7, 8		X		
	:9–10	X			
	23:23	X			
Mark	6:6	X			
Luke	4:18	X			
	10:7		X		
	:7, 8		X		
	13:22	X			
	22:35		X		
John	4:35, 36		X		
	14:26	X			
	16:13	X			
Acts	8:14, 25	X			
	:25	X			
	:15, 28	X			

	11:22	X		
	14:21–23		X	
	15:36, 41		X	
	20:28		X	
	:29		X	
	:30	X		
Rom.	10:15		X	
1 Cor.	9:4, 11, 13	X		
	:4, 12	X		
	:11	X	X	
	:13, 14		X	
	:16		X	
	12:28		X	
2 Cor.	3:6		X	
	8:19		X	
Gal.	6:6		X	
Eph.	4:11		X	
Philip.	4:16–18		X	
Col.	2:8	X		
1 Tim.	3:1		X	
	:7		X	
	4:14		X	
	5:17		X	
	:18	X		
	6:5		X	
2 Tim.	4:3		X	
	:5	X		
Titus	1:9		X	
	:11		X	
Heb.	7:4–9	X		
	:13		X	
	13:16		X	
1 Peter	2:5	X		
	:5, 9			X
	:9	X		
2 Peter	2:3		X	
	:15		X	
Jude	11		X	

Ready Way

1 Sam.	8:18		X	
Prov.	6:6–8			X
Jer.	22:29		X	

Brief Notes

Judges	7:20			X	
	:22, 23			X	
1 Sam.	8:6, 7			X	
	:7			X	
Ps.	105:15			X	
Prov.	24:21				X
Rom.	13:1			X	
	:3, 4		X		
2 Cor.	1:21			X	
1 Peter	2:13		X		

True Religion

Ex.	20:4, 5				X
Deut.	4:2			X	
Is.	44:18			X	
Jer.	10:8			X	
Ezek.	8:7–9, 12			X	
Habak.	2:18			X	
Matt.	23:15				X
Luke	10:41, 42			X	
	22:25			X	
Acts	17:11			X	
Rom.	14:		X		
	15:		X		
	16:17, 18			X	
Gal.	1:8			X	
Eph.	4:14			X	
Philip	3:15			X	
Col.	3:16				X
1 Thess.	5:21			X	
2 Thess.	2:11, 12			X	
Rev.	2:2			X	
	22:18, 19			X	

APPENDIX I

The pagination is that of John Mitford's edition of the *Works*, published by Pickering in eight volumes at London in 1851. The abbreviations employed are as follows:

Of Ref.—*Of Reformation touching Church Discipline in England.*
Pre. Episc.—*Of Prelatical Episcopacy.*
Rem. Def.—*Animadversions upon the Remonstrant's Defence.*
Ch. Govt.—*The Reason of Church Government urg'd against Prelaty.*
Apology.—*An Apology against a Pamphlet call'd A Modest Confutation.*
D. & D.—*The Doctrine and Discipline of Divorce.*
Bucer—*The Judgment of Martin Bucer touching Divorce.*
Tetra.—*Tetrachordon.*
Colas.—*Colasterion.*
Ten. Kgs.—*The Tenure of Kings and Magistrates.*
Ormond.—*Observations on the Articles of Peace.*
Eikon.—*Eikonoklastes.*
pro pop.—*Pro Populo Anglicano Defensio.*
Civ. Pow.—*A Treatise of Civil Power in Ecclesiastical Causes.*
Hirelings.—*Considerations touching the likliest Means to Remove Hirelings out of the Church.*
Ready Way.—*The Ready and Easy Way to establish a Free Commonwealth.*
Brief Notes—*Brief Notes upon a Late Sermon.*
Tr. Rel.—*Of True Religion, Heresy, Schism, Toleration.*

Gen.	1:27	Tetra.	4:144
	1:28		4:149
	2:18	D. & D.	4:23
		Tetra.	4:144
	2:23		4:144
	:24		4:144
	:24		4:211
	4:13, 14	Eikon.	3:493
	9:	Tetra.	4:150
	9:6	Eikon.	3:519
	14:	Hirelings	5:348
	10:10	Eikon.	3:527
	18:23, 25	D. & D.	4:73
	27:34	Eikon.	3:493

	28:22	Hirelings	5:352
	38:8		5:348
Ex.	5:	Tetra.	4:237
	9:27	Eikon.	3:494
	10:16		3:494
	18:15	pro pop.	6:45
	:19		
	:20		
	20:4, 5	Tr. Rel.	5:414
	21:	Tetra.	4:188
	:8	Colast.	4:370
	:18–20, 26	D. & D.	4:105
	22:17	Tetra.	4:164
	34:16	D. & D.	4:38
		Tetra.	4:164
Lev.	18:		4:217
	18:3		4:215
	27:3	Hirelings	5:352
Num.	5:	D. & D.	4:111
	12:7	pro pop.	6:45
	15:39	Tetra.	4:238
	18:21, 24, 28		
	:30–32	Hirelings	5:344–45, 352
	:28, 29, 32		5:346
	23:10	Eikon.	3:494
	30:	Tetra.	4:227
	35:31, 34	Eikon.	3:519
Deut.	4:1, 2, 5–8	Tetra.	4:216
	4:2	Tr. Rel.	5:407
	:5	pro pop.	6:45
	:5–8	Tetra.	4:179
	7:2, 3	D. & D.	4:41
	:3, 6		4:38
	:3, 6	Tetra.	4:248
	13:6, 9	D. & D.	4:42
	14:1, 2	Tetra.	4:179
	:23	Hirelings	5:345
	:24–26, 28, 29		5:346
	17:	Ten. Kgs.	4:461
	:8	Civ. Pow.	5:323
	:14	pro pop.	6:27, 46
		Ten. Kgs.	4:462
	19:5	D. & D.	4:105
	21:	Tetra.	4:188
	:14	Colast.	4:370
	22:	Tetra.	4:189
	:9, 10	D. & D.	4:47
	24:	Tetra.	4:188
	:1	D. & D.	4:21, 59, 80, 106
		Colast.	4:370
	:1, 2	Tetra.	4:175

Book	Verse	Work	Ref.
	:4	D. & D.	4:88
	25:19		4:64
	26:12, 13	Hirelings	5:346
	:18, 19	Tetra.	4:179
	32:4		4:178–79
Josh.	1:17	pro pop.	6:29
Judges	7:20	Br. Notes	5:392
	:22, 23		
	8:23	pro pop.	6:47
	15:11		6:76
	17:13	Eikon.	3:490
	18:24		
	19:2	D. & D.	4:111
		Tetra.	4:238
1 Sam.	2:12	Hirelings	5:360
	8:	Ten. Kgs.	4:462
	:7	Br. Notes	5:393
		pro pop.	6:47
	8:17		6:35–37
	:18	Easy Way	5:444
		pro pop.	6:36
	12:12		6:47
	:17		
	15:24, 30	Eikon.	3:494
	20:	Tetra.	4:185
	:8	pro pop.	6:42
	23:7	Eikon.	3:393
2 Sam.	5:3	Ten. Kgs.	4:462
	12:5, 7, 12, 13	pro pop.	6:42–43
1 Kgs.	12:16	Ten. Kgs.	4:462
		pro pop.	6:79
	:24	Ten. Kgs.	4:463
		pro pop.	6:79
	21:27	Eikon.	3:494
2 Kgs.	6:30, 31		
	11:17	Ten. Kgs.	4:462
1 Chron.	11:	Ten. Kgs.	4:462
	29:11, 12	pro pop.	6:39
	29:23		6:38
2 Chron.	15:3, 5–7	Ch. Govt.	3:136
	19:2	D. & D.	4:41
		Tetra.	4:250
	28:2	Eikon.	3:529
	34:33	Civ. Pow.	5:322
Ezra	9:2	D. & D.	4:38
	10:10, 11		4:38
Nehem.	13:24, 26	Tetra.	4:249
	13:30	D. & D.	4:38
Job	9:3	Tetra.	4:148
Psalms	17:2	pro pop.	6:41
	17:2, 3		6:41

34:	Tetra.	4:208
51:4	Ten. Kgs.	4:460
:6	pro pop.	6:42
73:26, 27	Tetra.	4:239
78:34, 36, 37	Eikon.	3:529
94:20	D. & D.	4:61
	Tetra.	4:218
	Ten. Kgs.	4:465
	pro pop.	6:34
105:15	pro pop.	6:34
		6:77
	Eikon.	3:520
119:138, 140	D. & D.	4:73
149:8	Eikon.	3:527
	pro pop.	6:40
Proverbs 1:20, 21	Ch. Govt.	3:148
2:17	D. & D.	4:52
	Tetra.	4:185
6:6–8	Ready Way	5:430
8:30	Tetra.	4:155
12:4	D. & D.	4:100
:10	Ten. Kgs.	4:453
18:3	D. & D.	4:2
19:10	Ormond	4:552
		4:580
21:9	D. & D.	4:100
:9, 19	Colast.	4:360
:19	D. & D.	4:100
:27	Civ. Pow.	5:331
24:21	Pre. Episc.	3:80
	Brief Notes	5:391
27:15	D. & D.	4:100
:16		4:100
28:15–17	Eikon.	3:327
30:19, 20	D. & D.	4:112
30:21	Ormond	4:551
:21, 23	D. & D.	4:81
		4:100
	Tetra.	4:183
Ecclesiastes		
7:16	D. & D.	4:130
8:1, 2	pro pop.	6:29
9:9	D. & D.	4:34
9:19	pro pop.	6:29
10:6, 7	Ormond.	4:552
Canticles		
8:6, 7	D. & D.	4:29
Isaiah 9:15	Rem. Def.	3:233
10:	Tetra.	4:218
:1	D. & D.	4:61
26:13	Ten. Kgs.	4:459

	44:18	Tr. Rel.	5:419
	45:1	pro pop.	6:77
	49:23	Hirelings	5:373
	52:7	Ch. Govt.	3:154
	54:16	prop pop.	6:72
	55:1	Civ. Pow.	5:324
	56:10, 11	Apology	3:307
	:11	Hirelings	5:360
	66:21	Ch. Govt.	3:117
	:23		3:117
Jeremiah	3:1	Tetra.	4:202
	7:16	Rem. Def.	3:244
	10:8	Tr. Rel.	5:414
	13:23	Colast.	4:359
	15:10	Ch. Govt.	3:139
	20:9		3:140
	:10		3:140
	22:29	Ready Way	5:453
	27:7	pro pop.	6:63
	29:24, 26	Civ. Pow.	5:322
	31:	Tetra.	4:199
	38:5	pro pop.	6:82
	48:10	Ten. Kgs.	4:451
Ezekiel	8:7–9, 12	Tr. Rel.	5:413
	13:11, 15	Rem. Def.	3:242
	17:	Tetra.	4:185
	17:9	D. & D.	4:53
	40:	Ch. Govt.	3:102
Hosea	7:14, 16	Eikon.	3:494
	8:4	pro pop.	6:59
	13:10, 11		6:47
Habakkuk			
	2:18	Tr. Rel.	5:414
Zechariah			
	8:10	Ch. Govt.	3:136
	13:4	Ormond.	4:571
	13:4	Ormond.	4:572
	14:20	Of Ref.	3:22
Malachi	2:11, 14	Tetra.	4:177
	:14		4:185
	2:15, 16	Bucer.	4:319
	:16	D. & D.	4:34
			4:88
		Tetra.	4:176
Ecclesiasticus			
	13:16	D. & D.	4:48
	25:26	Tetra.	4:177
	37:27	D. & D.	4:49
1 Esdras	3: and 4:	Eikon.	3:516, 517

Matthew

	5:18	Pre. Episc.	3:92
	:31, 32	Tetra.	4:198
	6:24	Eikon.	3:515
	7:22, 23	Pre. Episc.	3:84
	9:35	Hirelings	5:367
	:38		5:382
	10:7		5:376
	:7, 8		5:375
	:9–11		5:354
	13:26–31	Civ. Pow.	5:308
	:52	D. & D.	4:2
	16:17	Civ. Pow.	5:319
	17:25, 27	pro pop.	6:51
	18:6	Civ. Pow.	5:330
	:17		5:334
	19:	Tetra.	4:249
	19:3, 4		4:198
	:4, 5	D. & D.	4:85
	:5		4:102
	:4–6	Tetra.	4:210
	:7, 8		4:214
	:8	D. & D.	4:81–82
	:9		4:105
	:10	Tetra.	4:245
	:11, 12	D. & D.	4:86
	:12	D. & D.	4:110
	20:25	Ten. Kgs.	4:470
	:25–27	pro pop.	6:54
	22:20, 21		6:52–53
	23:15	Tr. Rel.	5:414–15
	23:23	Civ. Pow.	5:322
		Hirelings	5:353
	27:4	Eikon.	3:494
Mark	5:31	D. & D.	4:92
	6:6	Hirelings	5:367
	9:39	Civ. Pow.	5:310
	10:3, 5	Tetra.	4:177
	10:5	D. & D.	4:71
			4:88
Mark	10:7, 8	D. & D.	4:83
	:26	Tetra.	4:246
	:42, 43	Ten. Kgs.	4:470
	16:	Tetra.	4:225
	16:16	Civ. Pow.	5:325
Luke	1:51–52	pro pop.	6:50–51
	3:7	Apology.	3:290
	4:6	Ten. Kgs.	4:464
		pro pop.	6:59
	4:18	Hirelings.	5:366

:10	D. & D.	4:72
:12		4:72
10:15	Hirelings	5:382
11:	Ormond.	5:575
12:1	Civ. Pow.	5:332
13:	D. & D.	4:97
:1	pro pop.	6:57
	Ten. Kgs.	4:464
	Civ. Pow.	5:313
	Brief Notes	5:393
13:2	pro pop.	6:61
13:3		6:61
:3, 4	Brief Notes	5:392
:4	D. & D.	4:63
:5	pro pop.	6:61
:7		6:53
14:	Tr. Rel.	5:411
15:		5:411
14:4	Civ. Pow.	5:308
:5, 23		5:330
:6		5:326
14:9, 10	Civ. Pow.	5:327
16:17, 18	Tr. Rel.	5:415
1 Corinthians		
1:27	Civ. Pow.	5:320
2:15, 16		5:307
5:	Tetra.	4:150
:5	Civ. Pow.	5:334
:12		5:333
6:1		5:313
6:4		5:323
6:7	Tetra.	4:226
7:		4:228
		4:243
7:1		4:154
:6	D. & D.	4:43
:9		4:28
:10, 11		4:107
	Tetra.	4:247
:12	D. & D.	4:43
		4:44
:14		4:38
:15		4:35
		4:104
:16		4:44
:21, 23	pro pop.	6:51
:23	Civ. Pow.	5:327
:24	D. & D.	4:45
:25		4:43
7:26	Tetra.	4:155
9:4, 11, 13	Hirelings	5:378

4:14	Tr. Rel.	5:416
:14, 15	D. & D.	4:116
5:24	Tetra.	4:147
:30		4:167
:32		4:167
Philippians		
3:15	Tr. Rel.	5:417
4:16–18		5:375–76
Colossians		
2:8	Hirelings	5:386
2:8, 10, 14, 16	Civ. Pow.	5:327
:8, 16		5:326
:14	Tetra.	4:145
:16	Civ. Pow.	5:326
	Tr. Rel.	5:415
:18	Tetra.	4:147
1 Thessalonians		
5:21	Tr. Rel.	5:417
2 Thessalonians		
2:4	Civ. Pow.	5:307
:11, 12	Tr. Rel.	5:419
1 Timothy		
1:3	Pre. Episc.	3:76
	Rem. Def.	3:225
1:	Tetra.	4:195
:5	Ch. Govt.	3:105
	D. & D.	4:63
		4:82
1:5	Tetra.	4:254
:8	D. & D.	4:82
:18	Ch. Govt.	3:104
:20	Civ. Pow.	5:334
2:1	Ch. Govt.	3:104
2:2	pro pop.	6:65
2:12	D. & D.	4:100
3:1	Hirelings	5:382
3:3	Rem. Def.	3:217
:4, 12	Pre. Episc.	3:77
:7	Hirelings	5:367
:14, 15	Ch. Govt.	3:104
4:14	Hirelings	5:383
5:8	Tetra.	4:260
:17	Hirelings	5:365
:18		5:354
:21	Ch. Govt.	3:105
6:5	Hirelings	5:343
:8–10	Rem. Def.	3:217
:11		3:217
:13	Ch. Govt.	3:105
2 Timothy		
1:6	Rem. Def.	3:224

APPENDIX II

The pages are those of Sumner's Latin edition, printed at Cambridge in 1825, as this is the only edition of the original Latin that has ever been printed. The italicized pages are those that contain the reference indicated without quotation; but these have been thus indicated for the Old Testament only.

Exodus

31:10 p. 344.
31:11 p. 344.
31:13 p. 333.
31:16 p. 19, 29.
31:17 p. 29.
31:18 p. 29.
31:19 p. 343.

31:20 p. 19, 29.
31:21 p. 19, 29, 40.
31:27 p. 29.

32:4 p. 20, 142.
32:18 p. *78*.
32:27 p. *13*.

32:29 p. 532.
32:30 p. 532.
32:35 p. 489.
32:39 p. 17.
32:40 p. *19*, 429.

33:2 p. *134*, 155.

Joshua

1:6 p. *474*.
1:7 p. *412*, *474*.
1:8 p. *344*.
1:9 p. *474*.
1:17 p. 530.

2:4 p. *496*.
2:5 p. *496*.

4:7 p. *382*.

5:4 p. *277*, 329.

5:14 p. 87.

6:2 p. 87, *134*, 156.
6:21 p. *182*.

7:1 p. *183*.
7:9 p. 405.
7:11 p. *183*, 427.
7:14 p. 433.
7:19 p. 249, 433.
7:21 p. 467.
7:24 p. *182*.
7:25 p. *182*.

9:19 p. 430.

11:20 p. 145.

22:8 p. 533.

24:2 p. 237.
24:3 p. 237.
24:15 p. 528.
24:19 p. 19, 78.
24:22 p. 425.
24:23 p. *425*.
24:32 p. *480*.

Judges

2:   p. 533.
2:1 p. *91*.
2:18 p. *12*.

3:   p. 533.
3:19 p. *496*.
3:20 p. 394, *496*.

4:4 p. *340*.
4:18 p. *496*.
4:19 p. *496*.

5:7 p. 470.
5:23 p. 421.

6:11 p. 87.
6:12 p. 87.

6:14 p. 87.
6:16 p. 87.
6:17 p. 88.
6:20 p. 87.
6:21 p. 87.
6:22 p. 79, 87.
6:23 p. 87.

8:23 p. *472*.
8:30 p. *170*.
8:31 p. *170*.

9:1 p. 473.
9:2 p. 473.
9:23 p. 145.

10:16 p. *13*.

11:5 p. 485.

13:18 p. 21.
13:21 p. 77, 79.
13:22 p. 77, 79.

15:19 p. 199.

16:23 p. 77.

17:4 p. 435.
17:13 p. 435.

19:2 p. 177.
19:22 p. *490*.

21:7 p. 430.

Ruth

1:17 p. 429.
1:21 p. 17.

2:4 p. 516.
2:7 p. 516.

2:10 p. 492.

I Samuel

1:11 p. 425.
1:13 p. 417.
1:14 p. 497.
1:26 p. 432.

2:   p. 513.
2:2 p. 19.
2:10 p. *170*.
2:25 p. 148.

2:29 p. *440*, 478.
2:30 p. 23.
2:31 p. *182*.
2:33 p. *182*.

I Kings

1:4 p. 168.	8:11 p. *21.*	17:24 p. 152.
1:6 p. 513.	8:21 p. 296.	
	8:22 p. 418.	18:12 p. *471.*
2:3 p. 525.	8:27 p. 15, 132.	18:13 p. 471.
2:5 p. 489.	8:30 p. *132.*	18:17 p. 397.
2:6 p. *489.*	8:48 p. 248.	18:27 p. 494, 501.
2:7 p. 510.	8:54 p. 418.	18:28 p. 476.
2:8 p. 432.	8:60 p. 17.	
2:9 p. 432.		19:3 p. *364,* 460.
2:19 p. 514.	11:1 p. *171, 172.*	19:4 p. 410, 422.
2:23 p. *429.*	11:33 p. *77.*	19:10 p. 337, *440.*
2:24 p. *429.*		19:11 p. 21.
2:26 p. 526.	12:31 p. 413.	19:14 p. *337.*
2:33 p. 489.	12:32 p. *413.*	19:18 p. 337.
2:34 p. *489.*		19:21 p. 515.
2:36 p. *432.*	13:15 p. *481.*	
2:37 p. *432.*	13:16 p. 481.	20:16 p. *463.*
2:42 p. *432.*	13:22 p. *411.*	20:35 p. 412.
3:3 p. 415.	14:24 p. 464.	21:7 p. 528.
3:8 p. *525.*		21:25 p. *172.*
3:9 p. 525.	15:5 p. 169.	21:27 p. 424.
3:10 p. *525.*	15:11 p. 169.	21:28 p. *424.*
3:11 p. 416.	15:12 p. 490.	21:29 p. 424.
3:12 p. 416.	15:14 p. 169, 266.	
	15:19 p. *531.*	22:15 p. 494.
5:12 p. *531.*		22:19 p. 21, 79, 155.
	17:4 p. 143.	22:20 p. 145.
8:1 p. 88.	17:12 p. 14.	22:21 p. *133,* 158.
8:10 p. 21.	17:14 p. 143.	22:22 p. *119,* 145.
	17:21 p. 199.	22:47 p. 490.

II Kings

1:2 p. 406.	5:16 p. *472.*	10:16 p. 441.
	5:17 p. *437.*	
2:2 p. 515.	5:18 p. *437.*	11:4 p. 515.
2:4 p. *515.*	5:19 p. *437.*	
2:6 p. *515.*	5:20 p. 519.	12:3 p. 515.
2:9 p. 112.		
2:11 p. *372.*	6:2 p. *359.*	14:8 p. 475.
2:15 p. 112, 516.	6:17 p. 156.	
2:23 p. 515.	6:32 p. *502.*	16:1 p. 347.
2:24 p. 421, *515.*	6:35 p. 406.	16:2 p. 347.
2:25 p. *515.*		16:7 p. *531.*
	7:7 p. 501.	16:10 p. 413.
4:1 p. 518.		
4:15 p. 465.	8: p. 172.	17:2 p. *182.*
	8:12 p. 19, *28.*	17:3 p. *182.*
5:12 p. 241.		17:4 p. *182,* 431.
5:15 p. *472.*	9:30 p. 465.	17:13 p. 48.

17:14 p. 182.
17:28 p. 435.
17:33 p. 409.

18:2 p. *347.*
18:4 p. 436.
18:7 p. 431.

19:6 p. 441.

2:46 p. *170.*
2:48 p. *170.*

7:1 p. *170.*
7:4 p. 170.
7:14 p. *170.*

13:2 p. 525.

15:13 p. 413.
15:15 p. 413.

17:12 p. *16.*

1:10 p. *525.*

2:4   p. *449.*

6:12 p. *418.*
6:13 p. *418.*
6:16 p. 38.
6:30 p. 19.

8:13 p. *449.*

10:15 p. 143.

11:15 p. 435.
11:17 p. *171.*
11:21 p. *171.*

12:9 p. 414.

14:3 p. *436.*
14:11 p. 533.

15:1 p. *38.*
15:2 p. 38, 288.
15:8 p. *436.*
15:12 p. 191, 425.

19:15 p. 17.
19:27 p. 40.
19:35 p. *134, 156.*

20:1 p. *23.*
20:13 p. 467.
20:14 p. *467.*

21:6 p. 439.

I Chronicles

17:14 p. *16.*
17:17 p. *16.*
17:25 p. 421.
17:26 p. 421.

21:1 p. *145, 147, 159.*
21:15 p. 88.
21:16 p. 88, 156.
21:17 p. 88.
21:18 p. 88.

II Chronicles

15:13 p. *425.*
15:14 p. 191, 425.
15:17 p. *266.*

16:3 p. *532.*
16:7 p. 406, *502.*
16:9 p. 141.
16:12 p. 406.
16:14 p. 480.

17:9 p. 346.
17:10 p. *346.*

18:1 p. *531.*
18:5 p. *535.*

19:2 p. 479, *531.*
19:6 p. 525.

20:3 p. 460.
20:5 p. 418.
20:6 p. 16.
20:13 p. 418.
20:20 p. *102,* 405.
20:21 p. 533.

22:19 p. 247.

23:   p. 436.
23:26 p. 182.

24:5 p. 182.
24:10 p. *347.*

21:19 p. 88.

26:13 p. 433.
26:14 p. *433.*

28:2 p. 525.
28:5 p. 171.
28:6 p. 38, 276.
28:7 p. 38.
28:9 p. 19, 38.

29:2 p. 509.
29:14 p. 409.

21:4 p. 517.
21:10 p. 530.
21:13 p. 517.

23:17 p. *436.*

24:2 p. 168.
24:3 p. 168.
24:4 p. *414.*
24:6 p. *414.*
24:17 p. 528.
24:20 p. *502.*
24:24 p. 533.

25:7 p. *531.*
25:8 p. *531.*
25:16 p. 503.

26:18 p. 530.

28:6 p. 444.

29:6 p. 352.

30:2 p. *329.*
30:3 p. *329.*

30:6 p. *239*.
30:9 p. 248.
30:13 p. *328*.
30:14 p. 328.
30:15 p. 328.
30:18 p. 415.
30:19 p. 415.
30:20 p. 415.
30:22 p. 249.

31:1 p. *436*.

31:3 p. *449*.

32:31 p. 150.

33:8 p. *38*.

34:3 p. 515.
34:4 p. *436*.
34:30 p. 344.

35:20 p. *475*.

35:21 p. 475.
35:22 p. *23*, 475.

36:7 p. 414.
36:9 p. 347, 515.
36:13 p. 149, 431, *532*.
36:15 p. *48*, 53.
36:16 p. *48*, 53.
36:20 p. 447.
36:21 p. 447.

Ezra

1:7 p. *414*.

2:68 p. 509.
2:69 p. 509.

4:12 p. 363.

6:17 p. 374.
6:21 p. 329.

8:21 p. 424.

9:3 p. *424*.

10:3 p. *173, 175*.
10:5 p. 425, 433.
10:11 p. *172*.

Nehemiah

1:4 p. 423.

2:2 p. 460.
2:5 p. 472.
2:19 p. *363*.

4:4 p. 421.

5:8 p. 505.
5:14 p. *471*, 526.
5:15 p. 471.

6:6 p. *363*.

6:11 p. 475.
6:12 p. 535.
6:14 p. 421.

8:8 p. *346*.
8:9 p. 346.

9:2 p. 183, 249.
9:3 p. 344.
9:6 p. 124, *132*, 140,
        141, 155.
9:13 p. 162.
9:14 p. 162.

9:20 p. 111.
9:30 p. 111.

10:30 p. 425.
10:32 p. 447.
10:35 p. 433.

13:15 p. 447.
13:22 p. 393.
13:23 p. *172, 173, 175*.
13:25 p. 421, 433.
13:26 p. *171*.
13:30 p. *172, 173, 175*.

Esther

1:8 p. 463.
1:22 p. 512.

2:12 p. *168*.
2:13 p. *168*.
2:15 p. 459.

3:2 p. 530.

3:3 p. *530*.
3:4 p. *530*.
3:6 p. 528.
3:8 p. 363.
3:9 p. 528.

4:3 p. 424.
4:15 p. 424.

4:16 p. 424.

9:13 p. 490.
9:31 p. 424.
9:32 p. *424*.

Job

1: p. 158.
1:5 p. *236*, 469.
1:6 p. *134*, 155, *158*,
        159.
1:7 p. 157.
1:11 p. 422.

1:12 p. 158, 422.
1:21 p. 427.
1:22 p. 410.

2: p. 158.
2:1 p. 155, *158*.

2:5 p. *422*.
2:6 p. *422*.
2:9 p. 512.
2:10 p. 410.

3:2 p. 410, 422.

3:3   p. *422*.
3:12 p. *193*.

4:    p. 251.
4:18 p. 134, 154.

5:1   p. 438.
5:3   p. 408.
5:7   p. 142, 192.
5:12 p. 398.
5:15 p. 505.
5:17 p. 250.
5:31 p. 498.

7:11 p. 410.
7:20 p. 141.

9:8   p. 124.
9:10 p. 142.
9:20 p. 184.
9:22 p. *251*.
9:23 p. *251*.

10:8   p. 138.
10:9   p. *138*.
10:10 p. 138.
10:15 p. 184.
10:21 p. *193*.

11:7   p. 19.
11:8   p. 15, *19*.
11:9   p. *15*, *19*.
11:13 p. *239*.

12:1   p. *470*.
12:3   p. 470, 502.
12:6   p. 142.
12:9   p. 10.
12:18 p. 526.
12:21 p. 516.
12:24 p. 398.
12:25 p. *398*.

13:2   p. 470.
13:7   p. 493.
13:15 p. 400, 407.

14:4   p. 185.
14:5   p. 151.
14:6   p. 141.
14:11 p. 193.
14:13 p. 193, 382.

15:14 p. 185.
15:15 p. 19, 134, *154*.
15:25 p. 409.
15:26 p. *409*.
15:27 p. *409*.

17:12 p. 193.
17:14 p. 193.
17:15 p. 193.

19:3   p. 492.
19:6   p. *410*.
19:7   p. 410.
19:13 p. 485.
19:25 p. 205, 376.
19:26 p. *205*, 376, 377.
19:27 p. 377.

20:4   p. 16.
20:11 p. 515.
20:15 p. 467.
20:18 p. *505*.
20:19 p. 505.

21:7   p. 142.

22:2   p. 393.
22:19 p. 459.

23:3   p. 400.

24:23 p. *142*, 408.

25:3   p. *134*.
25:5   p. 134.

26:6   p. 19.
26:7   p. *134*.
26:13 p. 111, 127.

27:3   p. 111.
27:5   p. 399.
27:6   p. *399*.

28:13 p. 398.
28:14 p. 398.
28:15 p. 396.
28:20 p. 127.
28:21 p. *127*.
28:22 p. *127*.
28:23 p. *127*.
28:24 p. *127*.
28:25 p. *127*.

28:26 p. *127*.
28:27 p. 127.
28:28 p. *396*.

29:8   p. 470.
29:11 p. 393, *521*, 522.
29:12 p. 521, 522.

30:    p. 251.
30:1   p. *473*.
30:25 p. 482.

31:1   p. 465.
31:4   p. 141.
31:5   p. *400*.
31:6   p. 400.
31:9   p. 490.
31:10 p. *490*.
31:13 p. 517.
31:15 p. 138.
31:16 p. 521.
31:32 p. 523.
31:35 p. 400.

32:4   p. 515.
32:6   p. 515.
32:8   p. 135.
32:21 p. 498.
32:22 p. *498*.

33:4   p. 111.
33:18 p. 196.

34:14 p. 198.
34:15 p. 198.
34:21 p. 142.
34:22 p. 408.

35:7   p. 393.

36:14 p. 196.
36:26 p. 15.

38:    p. 134.
38:7   p. *133*, *134*.
38:12 p. 152.
38:33 p. 152.

40:14 p. 127.

42:2   p. 16.
42:11 p. *472*.

Psalms

1:1 p. 485.
1:2 p. 401.
1:6 p. 40.

2: p. 107, 214.
2:6 p. 59, 218, 219.
2:7 p. 29, 59, 77, *98*, 107.
2:8 p. 107, 380.
2:9 p. 219, 380.
2:11 p. 107, 408.
2:12 p. 107.

3:3 p. 251.
3:7 p. 474.
3:9 p. 420.

4:6 p. *459*.
4:7 p. 459.
4:8 p. 459.

5:4 p. 419.
5:5 p. 20, 146.
5:6 p. *146*.
5:7 p. *146*, 493, 499.
5:11 p. 421.

6:5 p. 194.

7:6 p. 136.
7:10 p. *18*.
7:14 p. 187.

8:6 p. *77, 134*.

10:3 p. 394.
10:5 p. 408.
10:6 p. *408*.

12:2 p. 493.
12:3 p. *493*, 498, 499.
12:4 p. 501.

14:1 p. 10, 394, 404.
14:6 p. 406.

15:1 p. 389.
15:2 p. *389*, 493, 504.
15:4 p. 430, 473, 499.
15:5 p. 508.

16:10 p. *196*, 376.
16:11 p. 20, 132, 384.

17:14 p. 251, 376.
17:15 p. *376*, 384.

18:2 p. *405*.
18:3 p. 405.
18:8 p. *21*.
18:21 p. 273.
18:24 p. 273.
18:25 p. *273*.
18:32 p. 18, *474*.
18:38 p. 489.
18:42 p. 532.
18:43 p. 489, 532.

19:2 p. 10, 127, 190.
19:3 p. *127*.
19:8 p. 20, 345.
19:10 p. 142, 348.
19:13 p. 274.
19:14 p. 403.

22: p. 222.
22:21 p. 196.

23:1 p. 466.
23:2 p. *466*.
23:4 p. 474.
23:5 p. 469.

24:4 p. 488.

25:6 p. 20.
25:7 p. 515.
25:9 p. 488.
25:14 p. 9, 396.
25:22 p. 420.

26:1 p. 287, 399.
26:2 p. 150.
26:4 p. 485.
26:5 p. *485*.
26:6 p. 488.
26:10 p. 527.

27: p. 405.
27:1 p. 475.
27:14 p. 407.

28:3 p. 499.
28:7 p. 405.
28:9 p. *420*.

29:10 p. 141.

30:7 p. 408.
30:8 p. 141.
30:12 p. 459.
30:13 p. *459*.

31:6 p. 201.
31:7 p. 479.
31:25 p. 407.

32:5 p. 249.
32:6 p. 417.
32:10 p. *405*.

33:6 p. 125, 127, *134*.
33:9 p. 16, 125, *134*.
33:11 p. 26.
33:12 p. 533.
33:14 p. 141.
33:15 p. 19, 138, *141*.
33:16 p. 532.
33:17 p. *532*.

34:8 p. 155.
34:9 p. *466*.
34:10 p. 466.
34:11 p. 466.
34:12 p. 408, *498*.
34:13 p. *498*.
34:14 p. 498.
34:15 p. 249.
34:19 p. 251.
34:20 p. 251.

35:13 p. 423.

36:7 p. 20.

37:1 p. 473.
37:3 p. 9.
37:5 p. 254, 405.
37:7 p. 473.
37:8 p. *473*.
37:12 p. 474.
37:14 p. 474.

88:13 p. *194*.
88:14 p. 420.

89:36 p. 205.
89:37 p. 205.
89:49 p. 196.

90:2 p. 15.
90:3 p. 250.
90:10 p. 151.

91:11 p. 155.

92:2 p. 420.
92:3 p. 420.
92:8 p. 142.
92:12 p. 489.

93:1 p. 141.

94:1 p. 489.
94:2 p. 489.
94:7 p. 408, 438.
94:12 p. 250.
94:17 p. 196.
94:20 p. 527.
94:23 p. 146.

95:6 p. 418.
95:7 p. 49, *438*.
95:8 p. 149, 438.
95:9 p. *49*, 438.
95:10 p. 53.
95:11 p. 53, 429.

97:7 p. *77*, *134*.
97:9 p. *77*.

99:6 p. 347.

101:4 p. 526.
101:6 p. 517, 526.
101:7 p. 495.

102:13 p. 15.
102:14 p. 420.
102:25 p. 15.
102:26 p. *16*.
102:27 p. 16, 382.
102:28 p. 15, 16.

103:2 p. 407.
103:8 p. *20*.
103:11 p. 20.
103:17 p. 20.
103:19 p. 142.
103:20 p. *134*, 155.

104:   p. 21, 134.
104:1 p. 20.
104:4 p. *133*.
104:15 p. 469.
104:21 p. 142.
104:29 p. 135, 141, *199*.
104:30 p. 111, 135, *199*.

105:14 p. 528.
105:15 p. 340, 528.
105:25 p. 145.

106:19 p. 435.
106:20 p. 435.
106:31 p. *272*.
106:37 p. 154.

109:2 p. 498.
109:6 p. 421.
109:28 p. 423.

110:1 p. 65, 78, 218, *219*, 224.
110:2 p. *219*.
110:3 p. *401*.
110:4 p. 214, 217, 429.
110:5 p. 78, 380.
110:6 p. 380.

111:10 p. 396.

112:5 p. 506, 509.
112:7 p. *405*, 474, *475*.
112:8 p. *474*.
112:9 p. *522*.

113:7 p. 516.

115:1 p. 409.
115:3 p. 16.
115:5 p. 436.
115:8 p. 436.
115:9 p. *405*.
115:17 p. 194.

116:6 p. 499.
116:12 p. 407.

118:6 p. *474*.
118:8 p. *406*.
118:9 p. *406*.

119:9 p. 515.
119:18 p. 345.
119:22 p. 471.
119:36 p. 467.
119:39 p. 471.
119:42 p. 502.
119:44 p. 402.
119:45 p. 277, 402.
119:46 p. 443.
119:51 p. 402.
119:55 p. 419.
119:61 p. 402.
119:62 p. 419.
119:63 p. 484.
119:66 p. 395.
119:68 p. 20.
119:69 p. 498.
119:71 p. 250.
119:95 p. 402.
119:98 p. 395.
119:99 p. 395.
119:100 p. 395.
119:105 p. 345.
119:106 p. 191, 425.
119:110 p. 402.
119:112 p. 402.
119:116 p. 407.
119:130 p. 345.
119:136 p. 460.
119:139 p. 440.
119:147 p. 420.
119:148 p. 420.
119:157 p. 402.
119:164 p. 419.

120:2 p. 498, 499.
120:5 p. 486.
120:6 p. 486.

122:6 p. 420.

123:   p. 405.

Proverbs

26:28 p. 498, 499.

27:1 p. 406.
27:2 p. 472.
27:3 p. 460.
27:6 p. 498, 503.
27:7 p. *136*.
27:9 p. 485.
27:10 p. 484.
27:13 p. *481*.
27:14 p. 498.
27:15 p. *512*.
27:18 p. 518.
27:22 p. 501.
27:23 p. 517.

28:1 p. 474, 475.
28:2 p. 533.
28:4 p. 479.
28:5 p. 394, 396.
28:6 p. 467.
28:7 p. 485.
28:8 p. 508.

28:9 p. 411.
28:11 p. 467.
28:13 p. 248.
28:15 p. 527.
28:16 p. *527*.
28:17 p. 489.
28:19 p. 469.
28:23 p. 503.
28:24 p. 504, 514.
28:26 p. 397.
28:27 p. 522, 523.

29:1 p. 503.
29:4 p. 526, 527.
29:5 p. 499.
29:9 p. 503.
29:11 p. 398.
29:12 p. 527.
29:15 p. 513.
29:17 p. *513*.
29:19 p. 518.
29:20 p. 461, 500.
29:21 p. 517.

29:22 p. 460.
29:23 p. 470, 473.
29:24 p. 458, 504.
29:25 p. 475.
29:26 p. 406, 529.
29:27 p. 479.

30:5 p. 396, 405.
30:6 p. 352, 396, 412.
30:8 p. 426, 466.
30:14 p. 505.
30:17 p. 514.
30:20 p. 464.
30:21 p. 175, 473.
30:22 p. 519.
30:23 p. 175, 519.

31:1 p. 526.
31:6 p. 469.
31:10 p. 526.
31:11 p. 512.
31:22 p. 469.
31:25 p. 469.

Ecclesiastes

1:4 p. *382*.
1:16 p. 470.
1:17 p. 398.

2:3 p. 459.
2:27 p. 467.

3:1 p. 399.
3:11 p. 399.
3:12 p. 466.
3:13 p. 466.
3:18 p. *196*.
3:19 p. 135, 196.
3:20 p. 196, 198.
3:21 p. *196*.

4:1 p. 469.
4:2 p. 469.
4:4 p. 467.
4:5 p. 484.
4:9 p. 527.

5:1 p. 411.
5:2 p. 418.
5:4 p. 427.
5:5 p. 427.
5:8 p. 505.

5:10 p. 467.
5:18 p. 466.
5:19 p. 466.
5:20 p. 466.

6:1 p. 466.
6:2 p. 466, 468.
6:11 p. 467.

7:1 p. 471.
7:2 p. 459.
7:3 p. *459*.
7:4 p. *459*.
7:5 p. 503.
7:7 p. 410, 505.
7:9 p. 460.
7:10 p. 352.
7:14 p. 402.
7:15 p. 142.
7:18 p. 142.
7:20 p. 184.
7:21 p. 476.
7:26 p. 512.
7:29 p. 32, *139*, 181, 398.
7:30 p. 500.

8:1 p. 529.
8:10 p. 408.
8:11 p. 142.
8:13 p. 142.
9:4 p. 142.
9:9 p. 466.
9:10 p. *466*, 470.
9:11 p. 143.
9:12 p. 175.
9:15 p. 510.
9:20 p. 396.
9:22 p. 500.

10:1 p. 497.
10:2 p. 516, 527.
10:3 p. 516, 527.
10:13 p. 527.
10:14 p. *527*.
10:20 p. 498.

11:1 p. 509.
11:9 p. 515.
11:10 p. *515*.

12:1 p. 515.
12:2 p. *515*.
12:3 p. *515*.

34:4 p. 382.

35:4 p. 99.
35:5 p. *99*.
35:6 p. 99.

38:3 p. 393.
38:17 p. 196, 393.
38:18 p. 194.
38:19 p. 194.

40:2 p. 251.
40:3 p. 93.
40:18 p. 435.
40:25 p. 19.
40:28 p. 19, 21.
40:29 p. *407*.
40:31 p. 407.

41:10 p. 474.
41:13 p. 475.
41:14 p. *475*.
41:20 p. 19.

42:1 p. 29, *104*, 106,
       112, 214.
42:3 p. 254.
42:4 p. 302.
42:8 p. 104.
42:14 p. 16.

43:7 p. 128.
43:10 p. 15.
43:28 p. 441.

44:1 p. 17.
44:3 p. 17.
44:5 p. 435.
44:6 p. 15.
44:12 p. *436*.
44:13 p. *436*.
44:20 p. 439.
44:24 p. 124, 138.

45:4 p. 33.
45:5 p. 17.
45:6 p. 124.
45:7 p. 124, 144.
45:12 p. 127, 152.
45:21 p. 17.
45:22 p. 17, 303, *431*.
45:23 p. 127, 303, 431.

46:5 p. 435.
46:6 p. 435, 437.
46:7 p. 437.
46:9 p. 17.
46:10 p. 26.

47:13 p. 439.
47:14 p. 439.

48:1 p. 414.
48:8 p. 185.
48:10 p. 250.
48:16 p. 111.
48:18 p. 534.
49:4 p. 338.
49:6 p. *222*.
49:7 p. *222*.
49:23 p. 528.

50:1 p. 46.
50:6 p. 222.
50:7 p. 476.
50:8 p. *476*.

51:4 p. 8.
51:6 p. 376, 383.
51:7 p. 442, 474.
51:12 p. 474.
51:16 p. 99.

52:5 p. *445*.

53:1 p. *204*.
53:2 p. *222*.
53:3 p. *222*.
53:4 p. *230*.
53:6 p. 223.
53:10 p. 205, 217.
53:12 p. 217, 218.

54:13 p. 260.
54:16 p. 128, 144.

55:1 p. 235.
55:4 p. 216, 303.
55:5 p. *303*.
55:6 p. 417.
55:7 p. 248.
55:9 p. 142.

56:2 p. *449*.
56:3 p. 303.

56:4 p. *449*.
56:5 p. 276.
56:6 p. *449*.

57:2 p. 535.
57:5 p. 194.
57:6 p. 194.
57:9 p. 434.
57:13 p. 534.
57:14 p. *534*.
57:17 p. *534*.
57:19 p. 132, *239*.
57:20 p. *138*, 251.
57:21 p. 467.

58:1 p. 534.
58:5 p. 423.
58:6 p. 423, 522.
58:7 p. 522.

59:1 p. 405, 421.
59:2 p. 421.
59:4 p. 393, 444.
59:15 p. 398.
59:21 p. 300, 349.

61:1 p. 112, 214, 215,
       488.
61:6 p. 340.
61:7 p. 251.
61:8 p. 457.

63:5 p. 104.
63:9 p. 89, 155.
63:10 p. 111.
63:11 p. 111.
63:15 p. *132*.
63:16 p. 437.

64:10 p. 249.

65:1 p. 235.
65:6 p. 32.
65:8 p. 485.
65:9 p. 38.
65:10 p. 38.
65:16 p. 429, 431.
65:17 p. 386.
65:20 p. 515.
65:24 p. 421.

66:2 p. 248, 409.
66:3 p. 414.

66:15 p. 375.   66:21 p. 303   66:24 p. *383.*
66:16 p. 375.   66:22 p. 386.

Jeremiah

1:5   p. 245.   7:16 p. *190*, 420.   17:11 p. 457.
1:6   p. 470.   7:22 p. 411.   17:21 p. 447, *449.*
1:7   p. *470*, 534.   7:23 p. 411.   17:22 p. *447, 449.*
1:8   p. *534.*   7:25 p. *411.*
1:17 p. 534.   7:31 p. 434.   18:6   p. *47.*
1:18 p. *534.*   18:8   p. *23, 240.*
1:19 p. *534.*   8:2   p. 480.   18:9   p. 23.
                       8:7   p. 397.   18:10 p. 23.
2:8   p. 535.   8:9   p. 535.   18:18 p. 414.
2:11 p. 435.   9:3   p. 498.   18:19 p. *421*, 534.
2:34 p. 505.   9:5   p. 495.   18:20 p. 534.
2:35 p. 403.   18:21 p. 421.
                       10:2   p. 439.   18:22 p. 421.
3:7   p. 248, 374.   10:8   p. *436.*   20:7   p. 534.
3:8   p. 247.   10:10 p. *14, 78.*   20:12 p. *490.*
3:12 p. 303.   10:14 p. 436.   20:14 p. 422.
3:13 p. 374.   10:15 p. 436.   20:15 p. 410.
                       10:21 p. 535.
4:1   p. *239.*   10:23 p. 144.   21:4   p. 533.
4:4   p. 248, 316.   10:24 p. 250.   21:12 p. 526.

5:    p. 534.   11:13 p. 434.   22:3   p. 526.
5:3   p. 148.   11:20 p. 489.   22:4   p. *526.*
5:4   p. 397.   22:13 p. 505.
5:7   p. 490.   12:1   p. 142.   22:21 p. 411.
5:8   p. *490.*   12:16 p. 429.   22:24 p. 38.
5:14 p. 535.
5:31 p. 535.   13:18 p. 502.   23:5   p. *219.*
                                             23:6   p. 100, 219.
6:8   p. 239.   14:11 p. *420.*   23:9   p. 440, 535.
6:10 p. 189.   14:12 p. *420.*   23:10 p. 440.
6:13 p. 535.   14:13 p. *535.*   23:11 p. 440.
6:14 p. *535.*   14:14 p. *535.*   23:16 p. 536.
6:16 p. *353*, 411.   14:15 p. 535.   23:21 p. 337.
6:17 p. 411.   14:18 p. *535.*   23:23 p. 19.
6:19 p. 411.   23:24 p. 16, 19.
6:20 p. 411.   15:10 p. 534.
6:30 p. 47.   15:11 p. *534.*   25:3   p. 182.
                       15:15 p. 490.   25:4   p. *182.*
7:3   p. 47.   25:5   p. *382.*
7:4   p. 414, 455.   16:4   p. 480.   25:8   p. 303.
7:5   p. 455.   16:7   p. 482.
7:7   p. *382.*   26:3   p. 23.
7:12 p. 414.   17:5   p. 406.   26:8   p. 364.
7:13 p. 190.   17:7   p. 254, 406.
7:14 p. *190, 414.*   17:9   p. 185, 187.   27:6   p. 432.
7:15 p. 190.   17:10 p. 19.

4:17 p. 251.

5:13 p. 534.
5:15 p. 248, 250.

6:9 p. 535.

7:4 p. 490.
7:5 p. 463.
7:11 p. 534.

7:12 p. *534.*
7:14 p. 239.

10:8   p. 400.

11:1 p. *346.*
11:8 p. 248.

12:2 p. 534.
12:4 p. 79.

12:5 p. *79.*
12:8 p. 506.

13:6 p. 407.
13:11 p. *422.*.
13:14 p. *376.*

14:1 p. *240.*
14:9 p. 146.

Joel

1:5 p. 239.

2:12 p. 423.
2:13 p. 423.

2:15 p. 424.
2:16 p. *424.*
2:28 p. 301.
2:29 p. 301.

3:2 p. 363.

Amos

1:3 p. 363.
1:6 p. *480.*
1:13 p. 532.

2:1 p. 352.
2:4 p. 490.
2:11 p. 533.

3:6 p. 144.

4:1 p. 505.
4:13 p. *134.*

5:7 p. 527.
5:8 p. 143.
5:11 p. 505.
5:14 p. 249.
5:15 p. 249.
5:18 p. 406.
5:21 p. 414.

6:1 p. 408.
6:3 p. *408.*
6:5 p. 414.
6:6 p. 460.

6:12 p. *527.*
6:13 p. 406.

7:10 p. 364, *535.*
7:13 p. *364.*

8:4 p. 505.
8:5 p. *505*, *506.*
8:6 p. 506.
8:11 p. 535.

9:14 p. 374.
9:15 p. *374.*

Obadiah

verse 10 p. 363.

Jonah

3:5 p. 24.
3:7 p. 423, *424.*
3:8 p. 423.

3:9 p. 423.
3:11 p. *24.*

4:3 p. 411.
4:10 p. 248.
4:11 p. 248.

Micah

1:3 p. *21.*

2:1 p. *505.*
2:2 p. 505.
2:6 p. 536.
2:11 p. 536.

3:2 p. 505.
3:3 p. *505.*

3:5 p. 535.
3:6 p. *535.*
3:11 p. 406, 527, 535.

4:1 p. *213, 302.*
4:13 p. 363.

5:2 p. 212, *213.*
5:12 p. 439.

6:6 p. 413, 414.
6:7 p. 414.
6:8 p. 414.
6:11 p. 506.

7:3 p. 527.
7:4 p. 502.

Nahum

1:3 p. *21*.

1:12 p. 15.
1:13 p. 19.
1:16 p. 408.

2:2 p. 343.

1:8 p. 465.
1:12 p. 408.

2:7 p. 213, 303.

13 p. 190.
1::10 p. 155.
1:16 p. *38*.

2:12 p. 143.

3:1 p. 88, 158.
3:2 p. 88.
3:3 p. *88*.
3:7 p. 297, 376.

4:10 p. 156.

5:3 p. 504.

6:12 p. 213, 215.

1:2 p. 52.
1:3 p. 52.
1:6 p. 408.
1:8 p. 427.
1:11 p. 446.

2:1 p. 535.
2:10 p. 125, 535.

Wisdom

11:17 p. *128*.

1:18 p. 112, 119, 212.
1:20 p. 112, 119, 212.
1:21 p. 215.
1:23 p. 81.
1:25 p. 126.

2:1 p. 439.

Habakkuk

2:3 p. 343.
2:4 p. 269.
2:12 p. 534.
2:15 p. 463.
2:16 p. *463*.

Zephaniah

2:1 p. *46*.
2:2 p. *46*.
2:3 p. *46*.

Haggai

2:9 p. 213.

Zechariah

6:13 p. *213*, 215, 217.

7:5 p. 423, *424*.
7:9 p. 482.
7:12 p. 149.

8:16 p. 493.
8:19 p. *424*.
8:20 p. 303.
8:23 p. 374.

9:9 p. 213.
9:16 p. *466*.
9:17 p. 466.

10:4 p. *533*.

Malachi

2:13 p. *512*.
2:14 p. 512.
2:15 p. 166, *512*.
2:16 p. 175.

3:1 p. 76, 90, 92.
107, 213, 214.
3:5 p. 506.

Maccabees

1:1:59 p. *344*.
1:1:60 p. 344.

Matthew

2:2 p. 439.
2:5 p. 219.
2:6 p. 219.
2:8 p. 499.
2:13 p. 364.
2:15 p. 346.
2:18 p. 128, 194.

2:18 p. 436.
2:19 p. 436.

3:3 p. *21*.

2:8 p. 442.

3:4 p. 535.

10:5 p. 533.
10:6 p. *533*.

11:13 p. 91.
11:15 p. 535.
11:16 p. *535*.
11:17 p. 535.

12:1 p. 135, *138*.
12:3 p. 363.
12:4 p. 374.
12:8 p. 77.
12:10 p. 92, 416.

13:2 p. 535.

3:6 p. 16.
3:7 p. 352.
3:8 p. 427.
3:9 p. 427.
3:16 p. *406*.
3:17 p. *406*.
3:18 p. 406.

2:7:28 p. 128.

3: p. 113, 221, 222.
3:1 p. 302.
3:2 p. 220.
3:5 p. 249.
3:6 p. 249, 321.
3:7 p. 406, 502.
3:8 p. 249.

Mark

10:38 p. 321.
10:42 p. 526.
10:45 p. 211.

11:23 p. 407.
11:24 p. 416.

12: p. 18.
12:28 p. 64.
12:29 p. 18, 64.
12:32 p. 18, 64.
12:34 p. 42, 64.
12:36 p. 113.

1:6 p. 274.
1:9 p. 434.
1:15 p. 245
1:17 p. 92.
1:19 p. 134, 155.
1:32 p. 107, 218, 380.
1:33 p. 219, 380, 382.
1:35 p. 112, 119, 212.
1:37 p. 16.
1:42 p. 212.
1:46 p. 136.
1:47 p. 136, 204.
1:68 p. 81, 204.
1:69 p. 81. 204.

2:6 p. 213.
2:7 p. 213, 221.
2:10 p. 459, 481.
2:13 p. 154, 156.
2:14 p. 154.
2:22 p. 213.
2:24 p. 221.
2:25 p. 113.
2:26 p. 113.
2:37 p. 424.
2:46 p. 367.
2:51 p. 221.
2:52 p. 211.

3:2 p. 322.
3:3 p. 322.
3:11 p. 520.
3:14 p. 533.
3:22 p. 114.
3:38 p. 276.

4:1 p. 112.

12:42 p. 392.

13: p. 373.
13:32 p. 72, 73, 97,
118, 373.
13:35 p. 463.
13:37 p. 463.

14:22 p. 323.
14:23 p. 323.
14:24 p. 299, 323.
14:25 p. 323.
14:26 p. 428.

Luke

4:6 p. 472.
4:16 p. 367.
4:17 p. 346.
4:18 p. 112, 215.
4:30 p. 364.
4:34 p. 158.

5:29 p. 469.

6:1 p. 313.
6:9 p. 187.
6:23 p. 364.
6:26 p. 472.
6:27 p. 478.
6:30 p. 509.
6:35 p. 506.
6:36 p. 20.
6:38 p. 509.

7:14 p. 198.
7:29 p. 322, 536.
7:30 p. 38, 229, 237,
322, 536.
7:47 p. 274.
7:50 p. 274.

8:2 p. 154, 314.
8:3 p. 314.
8:10 p. 346.
8:13 p. 240, 293.
8:18 p. 536.
8:30 p. 133.
8:31 p. 158.
8:41 p. 367.

9:20 p. 108.
9:23 p. 260.
9:26 p. 134, 154, 443.

14:34 p. 211.
14:36 p. 73.
14:39 p. 418.
14:62 p. 224.

16:15 p. 237, 301, 302,
317.
16:16 p. 38, 302, 317,
333.
16:17 p. 241, 333.
16:18 p. 333.
16:19 p. 224.
16:20 p. 152.

9:48 p. 409.
9:54 p. 441.
9:62 p. 42.
9:66 p. 402.

10:7 p. 357.
10:8 p. 357.
10:13 p. 43, 48.
10:18 p. 134, 158.
10:20 p. 32, 334.
10:22 p. 215.
10:25 p. 297.
10:26 p. 344.
10:28 p. 297.
10:31 p. 143, 481.
10:32 p. 481.
10:33 p. 482.
10:36 p. 477.
10:37 p. 477.

11:1 p. 75.
11:2 p. 75.
11:5 p. 417.
11:7 p. 292.
11:13 p. 114, 121, 238.
11:15 p. 158.
11:20 p. 98, 112, 121.
11:23 p. 187.
11:27 p. 485.
11:28 p. 9.
11:38 p. 321.
11:40 p. 415.
11:41 p. 520, 523.
11:42 p. 415.
11:52 p. 347.
11:53 p. 498.
11:54 p. 498.

John

Acts

20:33 p. 359.
20:34 p. 356.
20:35 p. 356, 426.
20:36 p. 418.

21:5   p. 418.
21:8   p. 355.
21:13 p. 364.
21:20 p. 483.
21:23 p. 425.
21:26 p. 369.

22:16 p. 321.

23:1   p. 399.
23:3   p. 502.
23:6   p. 194.
23:17 p. 533.

24:14 p. 5, 9, 255.
24:15 p. 376.
24:16 p. 9, 400.
24:21 p. 194.
24:25 p. 400.

26:6   p. 194, 376.
26:7   p. 194, 376.
26:8   p. 194, 376.

26:11 p. 441.
26:18 p. 189, 249, 268.
26:20 p. 249.
26:22 p. 300.
26:23 p. 300.
26:24 p. 398.
26:28 p. 238.

27:24 p. 24.
27:31 p. 24.
27:35 p. 443.

28:4   p. 497.
28:25 p. 113, 117.

Romans

1:1   p. 8.
1:3   p. 206.
1:4   p. 59, 112, 224, 225.
1:7   p. 71, 344.
1:8   p. 71, 75, 420.
1:9   p. 75, 420.
1:10 p. 420.
1:14 p. 341.
1:15 p. 344.
1:16 p. 301, 302, 327.
1:17 p. 301, 302.
1:18 p. 236.
1:19 p. 10, 190, 236, 295, 297.
1:20 p. 10, 14, 128, 190, 236.
1:21 p. 55, 407.
1:22 p. 397.
1:23 p. 16, 435.
1:24 p. 55, 147, 435.
1:25 p. 82.
1:26 p. 55, 190.
1:28 p. 145, 149.
1:29 p. 497.
1:30 p. 497.
1:31 p. 485.
1:32 p. 186, 190, 295, 485.

2:4   p. 148, 247, 406.
2:5   p. 148, 247.
2:6   p. 231, 273.
2:7   p. 231.
2:8   p. 383.
2:9   p. 192, 383.

2:10 p. 42.
2:11 p. 42.
2:12 p. 180, 379.
2:13 p. 9, 387.
2:14 p. 10, 42, 190, 295, 379.
2:15 p. 10, 190, 236, 239, 295, 400.
2:16 p. 101, 378.
2:20 p. 9.
2:24 p. 445.
2:25 p. 316.
2:29 p. 281.

3:2   p. 342.
3:4   p. 20.
3:9   p. 186.
3:19 p. 186, 188, 297.
3:20 p. 269, 297.
3:21 p. 269, 300, 303.
3:22 p. 229, 269, 303.
3:23 p. 184, 269.
3:24 p. 267, 271.
3:25 p. 204, 205, 214, 217, 228, 230, 267.
3:26 p. 267.
3:27 p. 269, 271, 272, 305.
3:28 p. 269, 271, 272.
3:30 p. 18, 269.
3:31 p. 308.

4:1   p. 272.
4:2   p. 270, 272.
4:3   p. 102, 255, 270.

4:4   p. 270.
4:5   p. 270.
4:6   p. 268, 270.
4:7   p. 270.
4:8   p. 270.
4:9   p. 272.
4:11 p. 316, 319, 320.
4:12 p. 310, 316, 319, 320.
4:13 p. 272, 307.
4:14 p. 307.
4:15 p. 300, 305, 309.
4:16 p. 307.
4:18 p. 254, 255, 257.
4:19 p. 254, 257.
4:20 p. 254, 255.
4:21 p. 254, 255.
4:25 p. 226, 231, 297.

5:1   p. 275.
5:2   p. 285.
5:4   p. 407.
5:5   p. 262, 287, 301, 407.
5:6   p. 229.
5:7   p. 229.
5:8   p. 84, 204, 478.
5:9   p. 230, 268, 286.
5:10 p. 66, 215, 226, 229, 230, 286.
5:11 p. 75, 230.
5:12 p. 181, 188.
5:13 p. 192.
5:14 p. 192.
5:15 p. 181, 203.
5:16 p. 181, 267.

7:21 p. 518.
7:22 p. 518.
7:23 p. 204, 311, 371.
7:25 p. 349.
7:26 p. 349, 426.
7:31 p. 383, 405.
7:36 p. 190, 349, 426.
7:37 p. 190, 426.
7:38 p. 392.
7:39 p. 172, 190.
7:40 p. 349.

8:2 p. 397.
8:4 p. 18, 65, 79, 116, 434.
8:5 p. 63, 65, 79.
8:6 p. 18, 59, 63, 65, 99, 125, 129.
8:7 p. 401.
8:8 p. 426.
8:9 p. 313.
8:10 p. 437.
8:13 p. 312.

9:5 p. 172.
9:7 p. 356, 392, 533.
9:9 p. 143.
9:11 p. 358.
9:13 p. 356.
9:14 p. 356.
9:15 p. 357.
9:17 p. 191.
9:18 p. 357, 392.
9:19 p. 313, 314.
9:20 p. 313.
9:21 p. 313.
9:22 p. 313.
9:27 p. 39, 289, 458.

10:2 p. 120, 318, 323.
10:3 p. 318, 325.
10:4 p. 318, 325, 326, 335.
10:6 p. 434, 459.
10:7 p. 434.
10:9 p. 89, 90, 111.
10:11 p. 343.
10:12 p. 288.
10:13 p. 20, 151, 255.
10:14 p. 434, 437.
10:15 p. 343, 360.
10:16 p. 325, 328.

10:17 p. 325, 328.
10:20 p. 437.
10:21 p. 325.
10:22 p. 438.
10:31 p. 389, 443.
10:32 p. 390.
10:33 p. 390.

11:3 p. 65, 107, 512.
11:4 p. 309, 419.
11:7 p. 162.
11:8 p. 162.
11:9 p. 162.
11:10 p. 156, 465.
11:17 p. 366.
11:18 p. 366.
11:19 p. 144, 148, 362.
11:20 p. 324.
11:23 p. 324.
11:25 p. 299, 326.
11:28 p. 329.
11:29 p. 329.
11:30 p. 324.
11:31 p. 408.
11:32 p. 250.

12:3 p. 115, 253, 301.
12:4 p. 121.
12:5 p. 121.
12:6 p. 121.
12:8 p. 347.
12:9 p. 241, 347.
12:10 p. 350.
12:11 p. 119.
12:12 p. 280.
12:13 p. 120, 243, 280, 321, 322.
12:27 p. 280.
12:28 p. 337, 338, 355.
12:31 p. 334.

13: p. 262, 456.
13:1 p. 334, 456.
13:2 p. 241.
13:3 p. 522.
13:5 p. 497.
13:6 p. 497.
13:8 p. 334.
13:9 p. 261.
13:12 p. 12, 133, 385.
13:13 p. 261, 334.

14: p. 345.
14:1 p. 340, 346.
14:3 p. 340.
14:15 p. 418.
14:16 p. 418.
14:20 p. 499.
14:22 p. 333.
14:26 p. 367.
14:34 p. 368.
14:35 p. 368.
14:38 p. 313.
14:40 p. 366.

15: p. 202.
15:3 p. 226.
15:4 p. 222, 224.
15:10 p. 388.
15:13 p. 231, 377.
15:17 p. 194, 230.
15:18 p. 194.
15:19 p. 194, 377.
15:20 p. 231, 377.
15:21 p. 192, 211.
15:22 p. 181.
15:23 p. 377, 380.
15:24 p. 220, 380, 381.
15:25 p. 380, 381.
15:26 p. 220, 380, 381.
15:27 p. 65, 83, 107, 381.
15:28 p. 65, 220, 381.
15:29 p. 195.
15:30 p. 195, 377.
15:31 p. 377, 433.
15:32 p. 195, 377.
15:33 p. 485.
15:41 p. 386.
15:42 p. 195, 385, 386.
15:43 p. 195, 385.
15:44 p. 137, 195, 199.
15:45 p. 135, 195.
15:46 p. 137, 195.
15:47 p. 195, 206.
15:48 p. 195.
15:49 p. 136, 195.
15:50 p. 195.
15:51 p. 377.
15:52 p. 197, 377.
15:53 p. 377.
15:54 p. 220, 376.
15:57 p. 220.

16:2 p. 453.   16:19 p. 361.   16:22 p. 370.

II Corinthians

1:1 p. 71, 337.	4:14 p. 101, 377.	8:13 p. 520, 521.
1:2 p. 71.	4:16 p. 234, 264, 385.	8:16 p. 481.
1:3 p. 20, 71, 75.	4:17 p. 231, 251, 385.	8:19 p. 362.
1:4 p. 252.	4:18 p. 255.	8:24 p. 390, 522.
1:8 p. 251.	5:1 p. 201, 233, 385.	
1:9 p. 251.	5:3 p. 201.	9:6 p. 523.
1:10 p. 251.	5:4 p. 202, 377.	9:7 p. 401.
1:12 p. 400, 499.	5:5 p. 202.	9:8 p. 522.
1:21 p. 74, 115, 284.	5:6 p. 202.	9:9 p. 522.
1:22 p. 74, 115, 116, 284.	5:7 p. 202, 255.	
1:23 p. 429.	5:8 p. 202.	10:3 p. 370.
1:24 p. 289, 362, 529.	5:9 p. 202.	10:4 p. 219, 370, 371.
	5:10 p. 202, 232, 377, 378, 379.	10:13 p. 470.
2:6 p. 369.		10:15 p. 264, 470.
2:7 p. 368, 370.	5:15 p. 226.	
2:8 p. 368, 370.	5:16 p. 434.	11:3 p. 499.
2:16 p. 230.	5:17 p. 100, 243, 244, 304.	11:5 p. 335.
2:17 p. 535.		11:8 p. 357.
	5:18 p. 83, 100, 215, 300.	11:9 p. 357, 358.
3: p. 305.		11:10 p. 357.
3:3 p. 301, 303, 349.	5:19 p. 83, 93, 100, 215, 230, 268, 300.	11:12 p. 357, 392.
3:4 p. 254, 256.	5:20 p. 100, 235.	11:13 p. 356.
3:5 p. 44, 189, 388.	5:21 p. 100, 217, 226, 230, 268.	11:14 p. 134.
3:6 p. 298, 299, 301, 303.		11:15 p. 134.
3:7 p. 303.	6:1 p. 39, 49, 263.	11:23 p. 392.
3:8 p. 303.	6:2 p. 49, 239.	11:26 p. 484.
3:11 p. 300, 301, 303.	6:3 p. 402.	11:32 p. 364.
3:13 p. 304.	6:8 p. 471.	11:33 p. 364.
3:14 p. 299.	6:14 p. 172, 531.	
3:17 p. 311.	6:16 p. 118, 281, 437.	12:2 p. 133.
3:18 p. 139.	6:18 p. 17.	12:4 p. 133.
		12:8 p. 422.
4:2 p. 346.	7:1 p. 262, 390.	12:9 p. 422.
4:3 p. 346.	7:8 p. 503.	12:10 p. 410.
4:4 p. 107, 149, 157, 189.	7:10 p. 239, 241, 248.	12:14 p. 357.
4:5 p. 337.	7:11 p. 248.	12:17 p. 357.
4:6 p. 100, 125, 128, 238.		12:18 p. 357.
4:8 p. 364.	8:1 p. 361.	12:19 p. 357.
4:9 p. 364.	8:3 p. 521, 522.	
4:10 p. 259.	8:8 p. 522.	13:3 p. 216, 342.
4:13 p. 253, 443.	8:9 p. 222, 472.	13:4 p. 224.
	8:11 p. 402.	13:5 p. 285.
	8:12 p. 401, 520.	13:10 p. 370.
		13:11 p. 265, 483.
		13:13 p. 120, 280, 301.

	Galatians	
1:1 p. 71, 74, 222, 339.	1:5 p. 75.	1:11 p. 8.
1:2 p. 361.	1:6 p. 235.	1:12 p. 8.
1:4 p. 75, 214, 226.	1:8 p. 333, 352.	1:17 p. 339.

1:22 p. 361.
1:23 p. 9.

2:4   p. 313, 484.
2:5   p. 313.
2:6   p. 339.
2:8   p. 335.
2:9   p. 335.
2:11 p. 314, 335.
2:16 p. 270, 271.
2:19 p. 259.
2:20 p. 230, 256, 260.
2:21 p. 270.

3:8   p. 270.
3:9   p. 270.
3:10 p. 270, 297, 305, 307.
3:11 p. 270, 298, 306.
3:12 p. 270, 297, 305.
3:13 p. 205, 217, 222. 298, 305, 307.
3:18 p. 307.
3:19 p. 87, 215, 297, 304.
3:20 p. 18, 66.

1:3   p. 75, 234, 259, 283.
1:4   p. 33, 34, 35, 261, 274.
1:5   p. 31, 34, 35, 36, 234, 276.
1:6   p. 35, 230.
1:9   p. 22, 30, 203, 207.
1:10 p. 30, 154, 203, 204, 207, 226.
1:11 p. 22, 31, 34, 35 36, 140.
1:12 p. 255.
1:13 p. 39, 114, 115, 286.
1:14 p. 114, 115, 286,
1:17 p. 65, 107, 238.
1:18 p. 238.
1:19 p. 224.
1:20 p. 94, 218, 224.
1:21 p. 94, 134, 218.
1:22 p. 218, 219, 281.
1:23 p. 281.
2:1   p. 189.

3:21 p. 298.
3:22 p. 229, 256,   298.
3:24 p. 7, 298.
3:25 p. 304.
3:26 p. 256, 276.

4:1   p. 304, 307.
4:4   p. 204, 206, 276, 310.
4:5   p. 225, 276, 310.
4:6   p. 115, 218, 243, 276.
4:7   p. 277, 311.
4:8   p. 14, 404, 413.
4:9   p. 449.
4:10 p. 449.
4:21 p. 304, 307.
4:24 p. 229, 304, 307.
4:26 p. 281, 304, 307, 353.
4:29 p. 364.
4:30 p. 304, 307.

5:1   p. 311.
5:3   p. 221, 316, 320.
5:4   p. 293, 307.

Ephesians

2:2   p. 149, 158, 189.
2:3   p. 185, 234.
2:4   p. 20, 35, 243, 245.
2:5   p. 35, 231, 234, 243, 245.
2:6   p. 231, 385.
2:8   p. 253, 270, 272.
2:9   p. 270, 272.
2:10 p. 244, 272, 388.
2:12 p. 296, 304, 333.
2:14 p. 296, 304.
2:15 p. 304.
2:16 p. 304.
2:18 p. 75, 115, 257.
2:19 p. 278, 281.
2:20 p. 335, 336, 343, 348.
2:22 p. 118.

3:4   p. 207.
3:5   p. 237.
3:8   p. 470.
3:9   p. 59, 125, 207.

5:5   p. 257.
5:6   p. 262, 271, 456.
5:12 p. 421.
5:13 p. 313.
5:14 p. 309.
5:16 p. 263, 265, 458.
5:17 p. 185, 263, 458.
5:18 p. 304, 307.
5:19 p. 434.
5:20 p. 434, 484.
5:21 p. 463, 484.
5:22 p. 253, 262, 306, 388, 456.
5:23 p. 306.
5:24 p. 458.
5:26 p. 471.

6:1   p. 368, 483.
6:2   p. 483.
6:6   p. 356.
6:8   p. 390.
6:9   p. 401.
6:10 p. 477, 509.
6:12 p. 414.
6:14 p. 265.
6:15 p. 244.

3:10 p. 23, 35, 134, 154, 157.
3:11 p. 23, 31, 35, 254.
3:12 p. 254, 257.
3:14 p. 75.
3:16 p. 284.
3:17 p. 262, 280, 285.
3:18 p. 215, 266, 283, 289.
3:19 p. 104, 215, 266, 283.
3:20 p. 75.
3:21 p. 75.

4:1   p. 366.
4:2   p. 366, 460, 484.
4:3   p. 366, 477.
4:4   p. 66.
4:5   p. 66, 86.
4:6   p. 16, 18, 66.
4:8   p. 86, 101, 219, 224.
4:9   p. 86.
4:10 p. 132, 224.

4:11 p. 338, 347.
4:12 p. 338, 347.
4:13 p. 281, 301, 338, 347.
4:14 p. 360.
4:15 p. 264, 281, 483.
4:16 p. 281.
4:17 p. 397.
4:18 p. 189, 397.
4:20 p. 263.
4:21 p. 263.
4:22 p. 184, 185, 263.
4:23 p. 234, 243, 263.
4:24 p. 139, 234, 244, 263.
4:25 p. 493.
4:26 p. 460.
4:28 p. 426, 504, 520.
4:29 p. 501.
4:30 p. 114, 115, 116, 286.

1:1 p. 354.
1:2 p. 76, 84.
1:3 p. 76, 264.
1:6 p. 264.
1:8 p. 429.
1:9 p. 399.
1:10 p. 399.
1:11 p. 387, 389.
1:12 p. 148.
1:14 p. 148, 444.
1:15 p. 415.
1:16 p. 362, 415.
1:20 p. 444.
1:23 p. 199.
1:29 p. 253, 444.

2:2 p. 483.
2:3 p. 470.
2:6 p. 85, 105, 107, 217, 221, 222.
2:7 p. 94, 206, 217, 221, 222.

1:3 p. 76.
1:11 p. 410, 460.
1:12 p. 232.
1:13 p. 141, 189.
1:15 p. 59, 61, 94, 107, 126.

4:31 p. 460.

5:1 p. 483.
5:2 p. 205, 217, 230.
5:3 p. 465.
5:4 p. 465, 501.
5:5 p. 465, 468.
5:6 p. 53.
5:7 p. 485.
5:8 p. 189.
5:9 p. 388.
5:11 p. 485.
5:15 p. 396.
5:17 p. 397.
5:18 p. 463.
5:19 p. 428.
5:20 p. 428.
5:21 p. 470.
5:22 p. 512.
5:23 p. 227, 281, 512.
5:24 p. 512.

Philippians

2:8 p. 205, 206, 221, 222.
2:9 p. 94, 101, 127, 223, 224.
2:10 p. 101, 127, 155.
2:11 p. 101, 127.
2:12 p. 238, 288, 408, 457.
2:13 p. 44, 238, 243, 388.
2:15 p. 277, 400.
2:16 p. 195.
2:17 p. 364.

3:1 p. 343.
3:2 p. 360.
3:6 p. 191.
3:7 p. 405.
3:8 p. 405.
3:9 p. 270, 273.
3:10 p. 231.
3:11 p. 195.

Colossians

1:16 p. 59, 94, 125, 126, 132, 133, 134.
1:17 p. 94, 100, 141.
1:18 p. 59, 61, 126, 219, 231, 281.
1:19 p. 103, 141, 281.

5:25 p. 227, 245, 512.
5:26 p. 243, 245, 317, 321, 326, 327.
5:27 p. 269.
5:29 p. 457, 458.

6:1 p. 514.
6:2 p. 514.
6:3 p. 514.
6:4 p. 513.
6:5 p. 518.
6:6 p. 411, 518.
6:7 p. 411, 518.
6:8 p. 518.
6:9 p. 517.
6:10 p. 265.
6:12 p. 158.
6:14 p. 360.
6:17 p. 349.
6:18 p. 416, 419, 420.
6:19 p. 420.
6:20 p. 502.

3:12 p. 39, 264.
3:14 p. 231, 390.
3:15 p. 266, 344, 348.
3:16 p. 348.
3:17 p. 536.
3:18 p. 536.
3:19 p. 189.
3:20 p. 195, 386.
3:21 p. 98, 195, 231, 385.

4:3 p. 32.
4:5 p. 76, 497.
4:6 p. 108, 416.
4:7 p. 108, 275.
4:8 p. 387, 395.
4:11 p. 466.
4:12 p. 466.
4:15 p. 358.
4:22 p. 263.

1:20 p. 154, 217, 226.
1:22 p. 217.
1:24 p. 231, 281.
1:26 p. 207, 237.
1:27 p. 207.
1:28 p. 265.

2:13 p. 83, 375.
2:14 p. 226, 228, 229, 245.

3:1 p. 530.

3:2 p. 488.
3:4 p. 204.
3:5 p. 204, 234, 243, 273, 321, 327.
3:6 p. 204, 273.

3:7 p. 267, 273, 277.
3:8 p. 9, 102, 387.
3:10 p. 369.

Philemon

p. 518.
verse 2 p. 361.

3 p. 84.

5 p. 102.

Hebrews

1:1 p. 87, 113, 216.
1:2 p. 59, 62, 107, 125, 141.
1:3 p. 15, 62, 100, 107, 141, 224, 229.
1:4 p. 59, 94, 107.
1:5 p. 29, 59.
1:6 p. 61, 77, 102, 155.
1:7 p. 133, 134, 168.
1:8 p. 81, 96, 107, 382.
1:9 p. 81, 107.
1:10 p. 59, 125.
1:11 p. 96.
1:12 p. 96.
1:14 p. 133, 155, 278.

2:2 p. 87.
2:4 p. 115, 119, 152.
2:7 p. 224.
2:9 p. 204, 205, 223, 226.
2:10 p. 65, 125, 276.
2:11 p. 95, 129, 277.
2:12 p. 277.
2:14 p. 206, 211.
2:15 p. 188, 311.
2:16 p. 206.
2:17 p. 211.
2:18 p. 211, 222.

3:1 p. 99, 216.
3:2 p. 95, 99.
3:3 p. 99.
3:4 p. 99, 125.
3:5 p. 99.
3:6 p. 99, 281, 290, 335.
3:7 p. 49, 113, 201, 238, 239.
3:8 p. 49, 239.

3:13 p. 366, 503.
3:14 p. 259, 290.

4:2 p. 241.
4:9 p. 448, 451.
4:10 p. 448, 451.
4:11 p. 451.
4:12 p. 136.
4:13 p. 19.
4:15 p. 211, 222.

5:2 p. 211.
5:4 p. 214.
5:5 p. 59, 214.
5:6 p. 59, 214.
5:7 p. 101.
5:8 p. 101.
5:10 p. 217.
5:11 p. 402.
5:13 p. 264.
5:14 p. 264, 399.

6:1 p. 8.
6:2 p. 8, 330, 449.
6:3 p. 8.
6:4 p. 234, 238, 289, 444.
6:5 p. 289.
6:6 p. 234, 289.
6:10 p. 232, 522.
6:11 p. 258.
6:13 p. 429.
6:16 p. 429.
6:17 p. 26, 284.
6:18 p. 17, 284, 285.
6:19 p. 285.
6:20 p. 285.

7:2 p. 219.
7:3 p. 95.
7:9 p. 181.

7:10 p. 137, 181.
7:12 p. 304.
7:17 p. 217.
7:18 p. 300, 304.
7:19 p. 300.
7:20 p. 217, 300.
7:21 p. 217, 300.
7:22 p. 226, 229, 300.
7:23 p. 328.
7:24 p. 210, 328, 329.
7:25 p. 210, 218, 256, 257, 329.
7:26 p. 185, 210, 212.
7:27 p. 210, 217, 329.
7:28 p. 210.

8:1 p. 218, 224.
8:2 p. 218.
8:3 p. 211.
8:5 p. 296.
8:6 p. 87, 300.
8:8 p. 219, 299.
8:9 p. 299.
8:10 p. 301.
8:13 p. 304.

9:8 p. 113, 294, 296.
9:12 p. 217.
9:14 p. 112, 217, 229, 245.
9:15 p. 229, 299, 329.
9:16 p. 299.
9:22 p. 211.
9:24 p. 218, 230.
9:25 p. 217, 329.
9:26 p. 217, 329.
9:28 p. 217, 227.

10:5 p. 75, 206, 211, 212.

II Peter

I John

INDEX OF BIBLICAL REFERENCES MENTIONED
OR DISCUSSED IN CHAPTERS I, II, AND III

BIBLIOGRAPHY

John Milton, *The Doctrine and Discipline of Divorce*, London, 1643.
ibid., London, 1644.
Pro Populo Defensio Anglicano, London, 1651.
De Doctrina Christiana, edited by Charles Sumner, Cambridge, 1825.
The Christian Doctrine, translated by Charles Sumner, Cambridge, 1825.
Photostatic Copy of the Original Manuscript in the Public Records Office. (Courtesy of Columbia University.)

BIBLES USED OR CONSULTED IN THIS WORK

Hebrew

Pagninus, *Biblia Hebraica*, (interlinear Latin translation) (Lyons, 1528.) Antwerp, 1584.
Münster, *Biblia Hebraica*, (parallel column Latin translation) (Basel, 1534–35.) Basel, 1546.
Biblia Hebraica, (Pentateuch only) Sabionetta, 1554.
Buxtorf, *Biblia Hebraica*, (Rabbinical) 2 voll., Basel, 1618–19.
Walton, *Biblia Polyglotta* (interlinear Latin translation) London, 1654 *ss.*
C. D. Ginsburg, Hebrew text only of complete Old Testament with many variants, London, 1906.
Rud. Kittel, *Biblia Hebraica*, (text only with many variants) 2 voll. Stutgart, 1912.

Greek New Testament

Beza, Geneva, 1589.
Walton, *Biblia Polyglotta.*

Latin Old Testament or Whole Bible

Vulgate, 6 voll., Basel, (Venice) 1498.
Vulgate, Leyden, 1524.
Pagninus, Hebrew with interlinear Latin translation, Lyons, 1528. (Antwerp, 1584.)
Münster, Hebrew with Latin translation in parallel column, Basel, 1534–35. (Basel, 1546.)
Leo Jud, *Biblia Sacra*, Zurich, 1543.
Vulgate, Tiguri, 1544.

172

Tremellius-Junius, *Biblia Sacra*, 2 voll., London, 1580. (Frankfort, 1575–79.)
Vulgate, Frankfort, 1585.
Tremellius-Junius, Hanau, 1596.
Piscator, (revision of Tremellius) Herborn, 1601, 1616.
Vulgate, Cologne, 1630.
Tremellius-Junius, Geneva, 1630.
Ibid. Amsterdam, 1633.
Vulgate, Paris, 1653.
Tremellius-Junius, Amsterdam, 1651.
Walton, Polyglot, London, 1654 ss.

Latin New Testaments

Vulgate, Editions cited for Old Testament.
Erasmus, Basel, 1520.
Tremellius, Syriac New Testament, Latin Translation, Paris, 1575.
Beza, London, 1577.
Walton, Polyglot Bible.

English Bibles

Cramner's Bible, London, 1562.
Bishops' Bible, London, 1573.
Genevan Bible, London, 1578.
   London, 1599.
   London, 1602.
   London, 1610.
Authorized Version, Barker, London, 1613, '11?
Genevan Bible, London, 1615.
   London, 1616.
Authorized Version, Barker, London, 1617.
Rheims Bible, London, 1617.
Genevan Bible, London, 1618.
Authorized Version, London, 1619.
     Norton and Bill, London, 1628.
     Barker and Bill, London, 1630.
Rheims Bible, Rouen, 1633.
Authorized Version, London, 1634.
     Cambridge, 1635.
     Cambridge, 1638.
Revised Version, American Edition, New York, 1920.

INDEX